Contents

Enlightenment
through
Aikido

The Founder of Aikido, Morihei Ueshiba.

合氣万生道の精神

合氣とは愛なり。天地の心を以って我が
心とし、万有愛護の大精神を以って自己
の使命を完遂することこそ武の道であ
らねばならぬ。合氣とは自己に打ち克ち
敵をして戦う心無からしむ、否、敵そのもの
を無くする絶対的自己完成の道なり而
して武技は天の理法を体に移ー霊肉一体の
至上境に至るの業であり、道程である。

The original Japanese version of these words was brushed by Aiki Manseido Dojo benefactor and calligrapher, Mr. Yoshito Nakashima. It hangs on the wall of the Aiki Manseido Hombu Dojo.

The Spirit of Aiki Manseido

Aiki is love. It is the path that brings our hearts into oneness with the spirit of the universe to complete our mission in life by instilling in us a love and reverence for all of nature.*

Aiki overcomes self. It not only takes hostility from our hearts but by transforming those who appear as enemies into enemies no more, it leads to absolute perfection of self.

This martial art, therefore, is the supreme way and call to unite our body and spirit under the laws of the universe.**

*banyuaigo no daiseishin: These are words that the Founder frequently used in describing the heart and spirit of Aikido. This translates as "a spirit of love and reverence for all of nature" or "a spirit of loving protection for all things."

**Ten-chi literally translates as "heaven and earth" but also can mean "universe."

The Founder and the author standing at the front gate of the old Ueshiba Dojo in Tokyo in 1956.

The Founder in prayer at Terayama Park in Kagoshima in October of 1963. Behind him is the author.

The Founder during a visit to Mt. Aso in Kumamoto in 1961.

The Founder teaching in the Manseikan Honbu Dojo in October of 1963.

The author explaining kokyu ryoku or "breath power" at the monthly yudansha training session. Once a month, these training sessions are held at Honbu dojo. Here each participant is given multiple opportunities to feel the author's technique and experience kokyu ryoku directly.

Translator's Note

This is the first of Kanshū Sunadomari's books to be published in English. The material in this book is taken from writings by Sunadomari-Sensei that appeared in his dojo newsletter between 1992 and 2001; they were later published in a book in Japanese entitled Aikido de Satoru. The reader should note that deletions, additions, and minor revisions have been made to facilitate translation into English. Furthermore, the differences between Japanese and English are significant, and nuances of meaning tend to get lost in the process of translation. Anyone seeking to objectively study and truly understand the words of the Founder of Aikido (Morihei Ueshiba) or Sunadomari-Sensei (or any other Japanese writer, for that matter) would ideally read their works in the original. However, not everyone can go through the time-consuming process of learning Japanese. That being said, even a perfect grasp of Japanese or a perfectly accurate translation would not ensure a full understanding of Aiki Manseido Aikido. Aiki Manseido, being a way harmoniously encompassing both spiritual and physical components, cannot be truly understood through words alone, however precise.

Over the past few years, I have had the great fortune to feel Sunadomari-Sensei's technique firsthand on many occasions. It is quite a bewildering experience. Grabbing the wrists of an eighty-year-old man almost half your size and instantaneously having all of your strength sapped softly and your balance taken effortlessly is both perplexing and humbling. Moreover, it has forced me to reconsider the assumed superiority of youth, physical strength, and reason, opening my eyes to the vast potential of spirit and mind.

It is my sincere hope that this translation accurately portrays the author's message and remains true to the legacy of the Founder of Aikido, Morihei Ueshiba.

Finally, I would like to express my sincere gratitude to Honbu Dojo shihan Katsuro Sato for his help, support, and explanations; Reverend Andrew Ellis for his encouragement and help; Samuel Lapalme-Remis for his assistance in editing and translating some sections of the book; and, of course, Sunadomari-Sensei for his instruction and guidance.

—DENNIS CLARK

Foreword

It is a great honor to have been asked by Kanshū Sunadomari to write an introduction to this English translation of *Enlightenment through Aikido*.

I first encountered Aiki Manseido, which was then called Manseikan Aikido, in 1975 when I was in my mid forties seeking something to "keep in shape." I enjoyed the experience so much that I felt I had wasted twenty years by not joining in 1953, the year Sunadomari-Sensei began teaching in Kumamoto.

Now, however, I believe it was perfect timing since I began just as Sunadomari-Sensei was rediscovering the true spirit of Aikido through the words of the Founder, Morihei Ueshiba, and in the process, changing his instruction of Aikido. The year after I started, "The Spirit of Aiki Manseido" was hung on the wall of the dojo, and we began each practice by repeating it, phrase by phrase, after our instructor.

I have experienced the change directly, especially in the last fifteen years, as techniques have changed. Of course, from the beginning the general principles of blending with an attack and then executing a technique have always been there. Sunadomari-Sensei would always say, "The purpose is not to yattsukeru [attack, defeat] or taosu [throw down] your partner or cause injury." Yet, more than that, what has developed in recent years is the spiritual aspect—that mysterious power that comes from a change of heart and mind to see the attacker not as someone intent on harming you, not as an enemy to somehow be fended off, but rather as a fellow human being that can be won over with love. Aikido as a way to take hostility from our hearts and make an enemy into an enemy no more—this is truly amazing.

This is why this new book of Sunadomari-Sensei's is so important, even revolutionary, in the world of Aikido, and why its publication in English is so meaningful today.

A phrase often repeated throughout the text is, "Aikido is both a martial art and a religious faith," which is what the Founder stressed. Unfortunately, much of the "religious faith" has been lost in the way that Aikido has been and is practiced both in Japan and throughout the world. In Japanese, the word is shūkyō, which can be translated as "a religion." However, an important point must be made here, which Sunadomari-Sensei hopes will be understood in the following way: The meaning is not that Aikido is another religion like the great religions of the world or the strange cults that often spring up from them. It is a religious faith. It is not a dogma or a set of beliefs or a form of worship. It is an all-encompassing belief in the victory of love and a harmony that unites our hearts with the loving heart of the universe. Call it god, or karma, or whatever, but it is living and continually challenges us to face up to the evil in the world and to do our best to help the good win.

As a Christian, I find that this Aikido is not in opposition to my faith, but complements and strengthens it. As I practice, words of my faith and biblical passages come to mind, like "Love your enemies," "When I am weak I am strong," "I can do all things through him who strengthens me." "The two shall become one [marriage rites]." "Overcome evil with good." Similar words and teachings are found in all of the great world religions.

I have experienced this change in heart, attitude, and practice through the help of Sunadomari-Sensei in practice at the dojo. It is not easy. I recall something he said to all of us shortly after I began practice twenty-eight years ago. "With diligent practice anyone can learn the techniques [forms] of Aikido in a year, but for kokyū ryoku [breath power] it will take a lifetime." That is even truer of "The Spirit of Aiki Manseido."

I would like to give another illustration that Sunadomari-Sensei has used in terms of "becoming one" with the other. It concerns the natural weight of the hand or arm as opposed to thrusting and pushing. A person is heaviest when completely relaxed, like being asleep or drunk. That natural weight flowing constantly and without effort into the point of contact with another person is the only way to become "one with the other." And you cannot possess it if you fear or hate your attacker.

Because it is not a competitive sport, Aikido has not yet suffered the fate of so many other martial arts. Many have lost much of their true nature and spirit because winning is the only goal, and to do that you must put the "other" down. Now, Aikido is challenged to return to its roots, to its original meaning and philosophy—yes, to its true spirit. The words written by Morihei Ueshiba many years ago have been preserved, and Sunadomari-Sensei has rediscovered them, bringing them to life through technique and giving them new meaning for today.

I hope that you will be renewed as you read this book, and that the love at the core of Aikido can help "bring your heart into oneness with the spirit of the universe to complete your mission in life by instilling in you a love and reverence for all of nature."

—REVEREND ANDREW ELLIS

LEFT TO RIGHT: *Fukiko Sunadomari (the author's elder sister), the Founder, the Founder's wife, and the author in front of the gate at the old Ueshiba Dojo in Tokyo during the Spring Training Session in 1956.*

Preface

"This budō is both martial art and religious faith."

The Founder of Aikido, Morihei Ueshiba, spoke these words directly to me in 1942, when I was his live-in apprentice [uchideshi]. Later that year, he said to me:

> *"This budō is a divine revelation from God. If you practice it for three months, you will have no enemies under heaven [tenkamuteki, which can also be interpreted as 'invincible' or 'having no rivals'].”*

Why did the Founder take the trouble to say these things directly to me when I was still only an immature youth? In those days, during World War II, Aikido was still called Aikibudō. More than a decade later, after the name Aikido had come into use, I was with the Founder and two other students when he said to us:

> *"However much one writes about it, however many things one says about it, one can never completely encompass this* budō. *This* budō *is beyond full description.”*

I think that these words clearly illuminate the Founder's state of enlightenment. Beginning in 1954, through fate and a personal connection, I began teaching Aikido in Kumamoto. In those days, Aikido was still uncommon, so many practitioners of other martial arts came to learn about it. Aikido is a martial art, therefore naturally many people wanted to test the strength of the technique. Immature and focusing only on kata [set forms], I felt that my technique had reached an impasse. How do I overcome this problem? It's not only physical technique. What is the spirit? From that time, I began to pursue the written words of the Founder regarding the spiritual world.

"Aiki is love. Aikido is harmony and musubi [connection/ unification]." How does one go about expressing this through physical technique? About twenty years after I began teaching Aikido in Kumamoto, I believe that I finally began to express these words through my technique. I felt deeply that this was the true spirit of Aikido, so I decided to recite the words of the Founder ("The Spirit of Aikido") at the beginning of every practice. [Translator's note: "The Spirit of Aikido" is the original title of this creed, as written by the Founder Morihei Ueshiba. It is now referred to in the Aiki Manseido dojo as "The Spirit of Aiki Manseido." The name change reflects the evolution of Sunadomari-Sensei's dojo and his understanding of Aikido.]

To attain true Aikido, we must make the written words of the Founder our aim during practice and in life. For that purpose, I decided to introduce the words of the Founder in the dojo bulletin. In these chaotic times, I feel deeply that these words are a warning to all of humanity.

"Aiki is a way of harmony. It is a manifestation of the natural form of all beings in which all of mankind and the universe are united as one. In other words, there is only one center in the universe, and it is the movement of this center that governs the world. The entire universe is one family. It [Aiki] eliminates fighting, conflict, and war from the world. It is a world of love—the world of the emotion of divine love expressed by the creator. Without love, nations, the world, and ultimately the universe will meet with destruction. Heat and light are also generated by love. It is Aikido that brings to realization this ideal in the actual spiritual world."

These words were written some fifty years ago by the Founder. Sixty years ago, the Founder said to me directly: "This martial art is religious faith. If you practice for three months, you will have no enemies under heaven." I truly feel that this is a big assignment given to me by the Founder. Somehow, I managed to solve it. Beginning in May of 1974, in the dojo bulletin I started to introduce the Founder's words, along with writings of my impressions and feelings at that time. In 1981, I published a book titled *Aikido no kokoro o motomete [In Search of the Spirit of Aikido]*. In 1985, I published Zoku *Aikido no kokoro o motomete [In Search of the Spirit of Aikido II]*. In 1998, through the Kumamoto NichiNichi Shimbun Information Culture Center, I published *Aikido Godo*. I truly appreciate North Atlantic Books for allowing me to publish *Enlightenment through Aikido* in English. I am also deeply indebted to and appreciative of the guidance of the spirit of the Founder, Morihei Ueshiba.

The Founder performing shihohai on the top of Mount Tatsuda in 1963. Behind him is the author.

My Mission

"The martial arts must be the path that brings our hearts into oneness with the spirit of Heaven and Earth to complete our mission in life by instilling in us a love and reverence for all of nature."

These words are a product of the Founder's divine inspiration from God. The mission of Aikido was bestowed upon the Founder from heaven. How many people alive today are living life conscious of their mission? In 1974, when I was around fifty years old, I became aware of my life's mission. Twenty years had passed since I began teaching Aikido professionally. At that time, I strongly felt that my mission is to spread true Aikido to the world, and that the words that the Founder received from God are the heart and spirit of Aikido. At once, I requested the late Yoshito Nakashima, a supporter of the dojo and a famous calligrapher, to brush "The Spirit of Aikido" (page x). I had this printed and distributed to each dojo and decided to have everyone recite these words in unison after me at the beginning of each practice. It took a long time for me to realize that these words are the spirit of Aikido. After many years spent overcoming pains and hardships on the path of life, one's own mission begins to reveal itself. In "The Spirit of Aikido" it is written:

"This martial art must be a path to complete our mission in life."

What is this mission of which the Founder spoke? Can we complete it? What is the true meaning of "completion"? I believe that once one has realized one's own life mission, he [or she] is already halfway along the path to its completion. Half of the journey can be thought of as the road of pain and hardship getting there. Eighteen years have passed since I made "The Spirit of Aikido" the purpose and focus of our Aikido training. At that time, at the halfway point in the journey, and now after another eighteen years, how far have we come? In February, April, and May of 1992, Manseikan Aikido put an advertisement in the Kumamoto Nichinichi newspaper. It read:

"In the twenty-first century, building a foundation for the realization of a world of true love and harmony: Manseikan Aikido."

Along with this mission statement, we printed "The Spirit of Aikido."* Why did we put out such an advertisement? After a chaotic century in which mankind crossed over many steep mountain passes and at the dawn of this new century, we must now confidently set a collective purpose and advance toward its fulfillment. With this spirit of love and reverence of which the Founder spoke as the foundation, we can make the world into a place of true love and harmony. I feel strongly that through the practice of Manseikan Aikido we can help build the foundation to make this a reality. Today's chaotic world was brought about by egocentrism and selfish desire. To extinguish this, transform

---

[*Translator's note: This creed was later re-named "The Spirit of Aiki Manseido"; the dojo has also undergone a name change from "Manseikan Aikido" to "Aiki Manseido." Because these writings are dated, the older name is sometimes used here.]

ourselves, and guide us to a world of true love and harmony, it is important that we physically express and manifest this spirit of love and reverence through our technique. This is the way of unifying body and spirit as described by the Founder below, and precisely the path we pursue in the study of Manseikan Aikido.

> *"By transforming those who appear as enemies into enemies no more, it leads to absolute perfection of self. This martial art, therefore, is the supreme way and call to unite our body and spirit under the laws of the universe."*

Presently, Manseikan Aikido appeals to many people as a path to the realization of a world of true love and harmony. This is the fulfillment of my mission.

FURIMIRU

In verbal as well as physical interaction, if people's kokyū don't match, conflict will arise.

JUNE 11, 1992

The Founder and the author in front of Lake Ikeda in Kagoshima, May 1961.

The Founder giving a lecture at the Manseikan Dojo upon his visit in 1961. On the left is the author.

The Founder during a demonstration at the Kumamoto Shinbukan in May 1961.

In past and present, there has been but one person given
the special seat of takemusu no bu. By means of the spirit,
you must resolve and endeavor to accomplish this mission
that you have been blessed with.

—SPIRITUAL INSPIRATION
RECEIVED BY THE FOUNDER OF AIKIDO, MORIHEI UESHIBA

To the People Whom I Have Had the Pleasure of Meeting on This Path

Dear Friends,

The season of Tanabata [a Japanese festival between July 7 and August 7] has come. I am delighted to hear that all is going well.

We are approaching the end of the twentieth century. For the human race, this is a very unusual time, occurring only once every thousand years. We have been blessed to have "received" the opportunity to live during such an uncommon time. Are you living your life consciously aware of this? Spending your time every day frivolously unaware of your blessing is truly a waste. In today's materialistic era, we have reached an impasse as we move toward the end of this chaotic century. Will the coming century be a mere continuation of the twentieth century? If so, the future of the human race is bleak. I believe that we are probably at a great turning point, one in which a change will take place from an era focused on the material to one focused on the spiritual. The Founder of Aikido, Morihei Ueshiba, stated clearly:

> *"[Aikido] is the path that brings our hearts into oneness*
> *with the spirit of the universe to complete our purpose*
> *in life by instilling in us a love and reverence for all of*
> *nature."*

A "love and reverence for all of nature" is at the very core and foundation of the creation of this new spiritual era. On November 23, 1953, I held my first public Aikido demonstration in Kumamoto city. Thirty-eight years have passed since then. During that time, on a long path filled with twists and turns and numerous trials and tribulations, somehow I feel that I have managed to arrive at a place where my technique fully realizes the spirit that the Founder left for us: "Aikido is the way of love." During these past thirty-eight years, through the practice of Aikido, I have had the pleasure of meeting many people, for which I am very grateful. When I first began teaching Aikido, thousands of people came into contact with my immature technique—some enrolled at various times, some quit practicing, many people experienced my technique. How those people felt about my technique at that time was a reflection of my technique during that period. Technique is something that matures and evolves daily. It has suddenly occurred to me to once again thank those people whom I have had the pleasure of coming into contact with, and to ask those who experienced my Aikido in the beginning to experience my latest Manseikan Aikido. Now, at the conclusion of the twentieth century and the dawn of a new one, I'd like to invite you to experience Manseikan Aikido again. Perhaps it can be useful for you as a method of unification of body and spirit. I hope and pray for your health and good luck in all that you do.

FURIMIRU

Even if you are shown the way, you cannot arrive
there without walking the path yourself.

JULY 11, 1992

The Founder at Terayama Park in Kagoshima, October 1963.

*The Founder standing in front of the signboard for the Manseikan Aikido Dojo,
May 1961.*

Even beneath a wonderful towering tree, in its roots lies a structure of struggle and perseverance.

—MORIHEI UESHIBA

Finding the Way

On August 15, 1945, Japan lost World War II. Amidst the rubble and scorched earth, people roamed the streets in search of enough food to get through the day. In those desperate times, all one could think about was staying alive. The Japanese word mugamuchu expresses a state in which one is feverishly and unconsciously absorbed in something. This word is an accurate description of most people's state as they were faced with survival. Several years later, after we reached a time of relief from this desperation, people began to consider "What should we do now?"

Forty-seven years have passed since the end of the war when Japan set its sights on rebuilding itself as a nation with a "high level of culture." Yet how is Japan viewed by foreign countries today? Japan may be seen as a major economic power, but on the other hand, culturally speaking, foreign countries may also think that Japan is rather colorless. A nation endeavoring to attain a high level of culture should first focus upon its spiritual culture. Around the end of the Edo Period, when Europeans and Americans came to Japan, how did they view the Japanese? Probably as a country with people of strong inner strength in which politeness dominated, and a nation that would continue to remain untouched by Western influence. Around this time, the term bunmei kaika [flourishing of civilized society] was born, and many people proposed the joining of Western knowledge and ideas with the Japanese spirit. After one hundred and twenty-five years, through several wars and many changes, we have arrived in the present day, seeking to further develop a materialistic society that makes people's lives more affluent. However, it is not a means for bringing about affluence of the heart. I believe that Japan's present condition is strong evidence of this. It is well known that Japan has become a society based heavily on automobile transportation. Many people have automobiles yet still don't feel a sense of satisfaction from this affluence. This is because owning an automobile has become a natural thing. When people view Japanese traveling abroad, they may think that they are wealthy, but on average Japanese don't view themselves as wealthy. The Japanese people are living proof that no matter how much money or material things people acquire, it doesn't lead to happiness.

Every day, throughout the world, tens of thousands of people are dying of starvation. Moreover, hundreds of thousands of people who have lost their homes in war and remain refugees are reported by the media daily. Due to modern transportation and communication, the world has become a smaller place, but unfortunately, there still remains a world of difference in the standard of living of the people of many nations.

All things living on Earth are given life through the working of one great power. All things on Earth come from the same roots, and a spirit of collective unity must come about. This spirit of unity gives birth to a spirit of love and reverence for all things. In the future, what is the fate of the human race? What will be mankind's final destination? Judging from the present condition of the world, a human race focused only on materialism cannot create a society of people whose hearts are truly at peace. Without the birth of a spirit of universal love connecting the human race, a material civilization is equivalent to nothing more than a magnificent structure built upon a weak foundation. In the words of Morihei Ueshiba, the Founder of Aikido:

> *"Through time the changing of Aikido technique is natural."*

> *"There is no set form in Aikido. There is no set form, it is the study of the spirit. One must not get caught up in set form, because in doing so one is unable to perform the function sensitively. In Aikido, first we begin with the cleansing of the ki of one's soul. Following this, the rebuilding of one's spirit is essential. Through the physical body, the performance of kata is that of haku [the lower self]. We study kon [the higher self/the spirit]. We must advance by harmoniously uniting the higher and lower selves. The higher self must make use of the lower self."*

The Founder clearly taught that the core of Aikido is the higher self or spirit. The path on which humanity must advance is the same as that which the Founder taught through Aikido. For humanity to reach its final destination, there is only one path that will lead us to a world of truth.

FURIMIRU

When listening, listen. When speaking, speak.

One's Own Mission

At the beginning of Manseikan Aikido practice, we recite in unison "The Spirit of Manseikan Aikido." Within these words is the concept:

"This martial art is a path to complete our mission in life."

Among those who recite this before practice every day, how many people can clearly answer the question when asked "What is your mission?" Looking up the word "mission" in a dictionary one finds: "a command for a messenger," "a commanded duty," "an extremely important assigned task," "a sacred task given to one's self," and "vocation" as some of the definitions. Thinking about the meaning of "mission" from a general perspective, it probably refers to when we are at work, doing our job earnestly and to the best of our ability. During our lifetime, it's good if we can enjoy ourselves while working; however, if one is working only to put food on the table, raise one's children, or build a home, can we say that this person has completed his or her "mission"?

Well, then, what is the meaning of "vocation"? Among the explanations of "vocation" are: "a divine duty," "an occupation awarded to one by God," "an occupation fitting one's natural, god-given character," "a duty that a person is individually gifted for," etc. Those who are divinely awarded occupations by God, like the Founder of Aikido, Morihei Ueshiba, are few and far between. Yet I believe that people who are gifted for a certain occupation or given a character that fits a particular occupation, can be seen everywhere. This is especially evident with people involved in handicraft or craftsmanship. I wonder if these people are doing their work consciously aware of their mission.

If we think about the meaning of "mission," first we must go back and examine the roots of why people were born on this Earth. If God is the creator of all things and put humans on Earth, there must surely be a purpose for our existence. God must have given each and every one of us a specific mission, "For the Earth, please...." For this purpose, we are nurtured and provided with all of life's essentials by God. Similar to a baby born pure, when the human race was born we too were instinctively at one with nature and must have lived life appreciative of all that is given to us. Over time, we came to believe that we could do anything and everything through our own power, and we have come to a point where we have forgotten the parent of the human race, Mother Nature (God). At various periods throughout history, to allow the human race to reflect and to caution us, people given divine missions from God are put on the Earth. However, the human race, caught up in selfish desires and pursuits, turns a deaf ear to God's warning and fails to recognize the damages it is causing by voraciously partaking of the Earth. We have now come to a point where it is often said that the Earth is in danger.

A rather prominent religious figure once stated: "The spirit of God exists in all things and pervades the entire universe, and man is the focus of the workings of Heaven and Earth. When God and man become one, infinite power will become manifest." Our true purpose is for man to unify with God and build a Heaven right here on Earth. Yet people's hearts and spirits have become tainted, and humanity continues to proceed on a course in pursuit of desires that take us further and further away from God. Therefore, from the heavens a true martial artist was put on Earth to help the human race cleanse itself of its impurities. On October 20, 1943, Morihei Ueshiba, the Founder of Aikido, received the following words as a divine inspiration from God:

"In past and present, there has been but one person given the special seat of takemusu no bu. By means of the spirit, you must resolve and endeavor to accomplish this mission that you have been blessed with."

After the end of World War II, through a new "Aikido," Morihei Ueshiba began purifying himself through technique. Among the Founder's poems is the following:

Grand techniques of ki:
Bringing calm to the spirit,
tools of purification.
Kindly offer us guidance,
God of Heaven and Earth.

In the morning and evening of each day, the Founder devoted himself in prayer to God. Twenty-three years have elapsed since the Founder passed to Heaven. Since that time the world has become more and more chaotic and directionless. The mission of the practice of Aikido is clearly defined:

"Aiki is the way of love. It is the path that brings our hearts into oneness with the spirit of the universe to complete our mission in life by instilling in us a love and reverence for all of nature."

The "spirit of the universe" is universal, all-encompassing love, the love of God. Through this all-encompassing love, all things in nature evolve. For humans, by connecting with this spirit of universal love, we instill in ourselves a love and reverence for all of nature, thereby unifying ourselves with all things. This is the important point for becoming aware of our own mission in life. The goal of the human race is to build a paradise on Earth, and each individual's mission is to make the most of their abilities helping to bring about the accomplishment of this goal. Manseikan Aikido exists for the purpose of unifying body and spirit and creating a firm foundation for the realization and achievement of our collective purpose.

FURIMIRU

When you feel the urge to speak unkindly of others, foster a heart that remains tight-lipped. When others speak unkindly of you, foster a heart that turns a deaf ear.

SEPTEMBER 11, 1992

Worry not about future pains and troubles for this only serves to tire the body and the spirit; empty your mind and don't be burdened.

—MORIHEI UESHIBA

Taking Hostility from Our Hearts

At the beginning of each practice, we recite the "Spirit of Manseikan Aikido." In it is a sentence that reads "It (aiki) not only takes hostility from our hearts, but transforms those who appear as enemies into enemies no more." In simple terms, an enemy refers to a entity with whom someone is in conflict with or an "opponent" in a quarrel or fight. If one thinks about the basic concept of "enemy," on a small scale it can refer to conflict between individuals or on a much larger scale it can involve conflicts between different groups, races, countries, etc. Yet, just what exactly does it mean to "take hostility from our hearts" and "to transform those who appear as enemies into enemies no more"?

There are wars occurring in various locations throughout the world today. As a result, everyday many people are victimized, injured, and die. Why do wars such as these occur? Racial conflict, religious strife, differences in thinking style, and economic factors are all among the various problems that lie at the root of this bloodshed and violence. The "I am right you are wrong" way of thinking and forcing another person to submit to one's own will contribute further to the conflict that exists in the world today. Just as wars have been fought using solely "economic means," fighting is not necessarily limited to using just physical violence for attainment of one's own selfish desires. In a world such as this, is it really possible to take hostility from our hearts and free ourselves from animosity?

"Taking hostility from our hearts" doesn't mean unwillingly submitting ourselves to someone else. And by forcibly making others submit to you it only serves to foster grudges and invite revenge upon yourself at some later date. Because the sentence continues with, "transforming those who appear as enemies enemies no more," to accomplish this it is essential that we lead this so-called "enemy" around to see our way of thinking enabling us to extinguish the feeling of hostility within their hearts as well.

Why is it that in our modern times, there still exists so much conflict? This is without a doubt due to the fact that peoples' hearts have become increasingly self-centered. The "as long as I am okay, who cares about others" philosophy is much to blame for this. The world today is full of contradictions. Due to extravagance, there are countries that produce a mountain of leftovers, yet at the same time, there are countries in which many people are without food and die of starvation daily. The positive effects of continuing scientific advancement and the transformation of society through modern technology has lead many people to say that the world is becoming smaller and more unified. However, if the hearts of the people of the world remain scattered we will be eternally without peace in this world.

The founder of Aikido, Morihei Ueshiba, was inspired by God to create for all people not technique which is used to down your partner, but rather technique to extinguish animosity and cultivate a world of love. The basis of this divine mission he received through enlightenment and ultimately the mission of all martial arts (Budō), is to stop conflict before it occurs and build a peaceful world on earth.

One of the Founder's poems reads:

> Set in motion
> the power of the cosmos
> by wielding Aiki:
> Create a beautiful world,
> and foster peacefulness

If we do not reach the point at which every individual fosters this spirit of which the Founder spoke, free from animosity and free from the perception of enemies, the world can never be truly at peace. No matter how wonderful of a system (government, education, etc.) is created, if peoples' hearts do not become good-natured a truly wonderful world will not be realized.

It is written in the Spirit of Aikido: "Aiki is love. It is the path that brings our hearts into oneness with the spirit of the universe to complete our mission in life by instilling in us a love and reverence for all of nature."

This "spirit of the universe" is unconditional love. The love that exists in nature and fosters all of life. The Founder's words point to awakening this love within us, fostering it towards all living things, and using all of our abilities to achieve our utmost potential.

Aikido is not technique for destroying. It is a teaching of the way of mutual prosperity by absorbing the spirit of our partner, connecting with him/her, and becoming one. It is a way to remove hostility from our hearts through the practice of physical technique and by doing so leads us to unification of body and spirit.

Among his teachings, the Founder proclaims that all technique must be guided by and embody the spirit, and he urges us to polish and refine our spirit. The techniques of Manseikan Aikido in which we give ourselves completely to our partner—thereby harmoniously connecting with him—are just that.

OCTOBER 11, 1992

"Aikido" brushed by the Founder.

Takemusu is the generation of spontaneous martial techniques by remaining in accordance with the power and structure of nature.

—MORIHEI UESHIBA

What Is Takemusu Aiki?

On a wall of the Manseikan Headquarters Dojo hangs a scroll that reads "Takemusu Aiki." The Founder of Aikido brushed this scroll in Tokyo and sent it to the Manseikan Dojo for the occasion of his visit to Kumamoto in 1961. Because I received this work from the Founder himself, I proudly display it on the dojo wall to this day. Yet this has in the past been reminiscent of the Japanese proverb "casting pearls before swine." It is to my deep regret that as an unworthy pupil of a great teacher, during much of the thirty-odd years that the scroll hung there, I remained unaware of its profound significance. Yet somehow, over time, I managed to realize its deeper meaning. As my understanding deepened, the level of my technique progressed to the point where it expresses the meaning of the words.

When did the words "takemusu aiki" come to him, and when did the Founder begin using them? Recently, after researching this

---

[Translator's Note: The words "Takemusu Aiki" are composed of four kanji characters. Take—also pronounced bu—is a character that has the arguably closest meaning in English to "martial." Musu means to "spring forth" or "give birth to." Aiki is of course made up of the same characters used in the word "aikido." Aiki is often translated as "unifying or harmonizing of energy/force."]

question, I learned that the Founder received this revelation from God sometime in 1942. However, in just what form and how this revelation was passed on to him are not precisely known. The word takemusu was among the many signs given to the Founder from Sarutahiko Ō-kami (the gods that serve as guardians for the community). Taking a look at a few of these revelations, perhaps we can attempt to awaken ourselves to the deeper meaning behind them.

- In past and present, there has been but one person given the special seat of Takemusu no Bu. By means of the spirit, thou must resolve and endeavor to accomplish this mission that thou hast been blessed with.

- Having completely withdrawn yourself from the system and practice of martial arts based on the lower self, and in that year of retirement having undergone your destiny of receiving the mission of takemusu from God, you must discard the lower self, dedicate yourself to mastering the higher self, and appreciate the art of takemusu.

- Unarmed battle is the enlivenment of the spirit; mastery of the art of takemusu begins here.

- Break old forms and craft new forms free of form. Continuously giving birth to new forms generated in response to the situation at hand, this is the heart of takemusu. Harmoniously connecting with natural and universal ki is essential.

- Takemusu is the generation of spontaneous martial techniques by remaining in accordance with the power and structure of nature. It is constantly giving birth to new creations.

- All people, give the spirit of love to the void and embrace everything! This is takemusu.

- Even with a seed, if the earth does not absorb love there will be no growth. Therefore, link the original vast ki of love, and through the ki of love of takemusu, give birth to techniques. The result will not be a temporary mechanism, but the birth of the power of divine techniques.

- Being trapped by the values of the lower self, feeling restlessness, confusion of the heart, obsession with material things, being vexed by worldly cares—all of these have nothing to do with takemusu.

- The essence of takemusu is the creation of infinite, universal variation in accordance with the laws of Heaven and Earth.

- The art of takemusu emphasizes spirit over form. Fundamentally, giving life to the spirit, through martial arts, will link your spirit to the love of the Great God.

- The martial arts are given life through constant change. Takemusu is giving birth to endless innovation evermore.

- We must break from set form, create, generate, and evolve. Takemusu is both vast and subtle.

- When teaching the martial arts, make sure to speak in terms of takemusu.

- The true martial art is that which reveals the meaning of takemusu.

- For takemusu, you must have true freedom of will. The lower self will reach its limits.

- Giving rise to the spirit: with freedom, it has no limits. This is the secret of takemusu. The secret of martial arts has no set form; instead it is giving free rein to the spirit. This is the secret.

- Do away with set forms. With the mastery of spirit as your highest principle, pour your heart and soul into the art of takemusu, and seek [the truth]. If you waver from making the spirit the center of your existence, all techniques and movements are of no use.

- Because the lower self is essential for the physical body, because revelation of the truth and activation of the spirit are expressed through the lower self, and because the body and spirit become one and give birth to change in the martial arts, the lower self cannot be dismissed. However, although I command you to reverse the lower self's precedence over the spirit and to correct this contradiction, do not take this to mean that the lower self is unnecessary. The lower self is of definite importance.

- Until today, there was no one given the divine mission through the martial arts; as did Ueshiba, be moved to tears and devote yourself.

The periods during which the Founder received his divine revelations were extremely grueling for him. It appears that many of these revelations came to him during World War II, the period of greatest mental, physical, and spiritual fatigue in his life. These years were particularly difficult for him because he had been forced to act against his better intentions in a few incidents due to his position. Having overcome these difficulties, he was inspired by God. He was warned that the lower self/physical element was not of ultimate value, and that he must devote himself and put all of his efforts into the spiritual.

In 1942 when I was living in the dojo as one of the Founder's apprentices, one day he told me gently, "This budō is a divine revelation from God. If you practice it for three months, you will have no enemies under heaven." I clearly remember him saying this to me as if it were only yesterday. As a young boy still in my teens, there was no way I could have possibly grasped the deeper meaning behind these words. The Founder presented me with a great riddle, which after fifty years, I have now finally come to understand.

FURIMIRU

Appreciating something after it is already gone is
too late.

NOVEMBER 11, 1992

*"Takemusu Aiki" brushed by the Founder
and given to the author and the Manseikan dojo in 1961.
This work hangs on the wall of the Aiki Manseido Honbu dojo.*

The Founder demonstrating at the Shinbukan Dojo in Kumamoto City in 1961.

The martial arts are given life through constant change.
Takemusu is giving birth to endless innovation evermore.

—MORIHEI UESHIBA

The Mission of Takemusu Aiki

The Founder of Aikido, Morihei Ueshiba, stated:

> *"The 'Aiki' of which conventional martial artists spoke and the 'Aiki' of which I speak are fundamentally different in both essence and substance. It is my sincere hope that you will ponder this deeply."*

He further stated:

> *"Aikido is not the art of fighting using brute strength or deadly weapons, or the use of physical power or deadly weapons to destroy one's enemies, but a way of harmonizing the world and unifying the human race as one family. It is a path of service that works through the spirit of God's love and universal harmony by the fulfillment of each individual's respective role. This way is the way of the universe; the training in Aiki is training in divine technique. Begin to put this into practice, and the power of the universe will come forth and you will be in accord with the universe itself."*

I feel that in these brief descriptions by the Founder, the purpose and aim of Takemusu Aiki can be understood. Simply espousing such things is easy, but expressing this spirit and bringing it to life through physical techniques is quite difficult. The Founder goes on to explain further:

> *"Aikido is the realization of infinite power and making it a part of oneself. Aiki is the power of the spirit. The power of the spirit—we must study and train to realize this."*

The explanations by the Founder are straightforward, but the fulfillment of this way must develop individually and distinctively, according to the receiver. "The Aiki of which I speak is different in both essence and substance from that of which others speak." By this, the Founder clearly means that his "Aiki" is Takemusu Aiki and is a mission bestowed upon him by Ō-kami [God]. As I have written in previous issues, takemusu is the martial art that was brought down from the heavens by Sarutahiko Ō-kami [the gods that serve as guardians for the community]. It was also at this time that the name Tsunemori was bestowed upon the Founder.* This was on January 21, 1953.

Around 1955, the number of Aikido practitioners greatly increased. From that period on, when the Founder lectured during training, his instruction placed emphasis mainly on the spiritual instead of physical technique. Many of those who came to practice preferred physical technique to lectures, so a large number of them tended to flow toward the practice times of the younger instructors. The Founder profoundly wished that everyone would understand the "bu" of takemusu that he received from God. Because of this, naturally the majority of his instruction and lectures came to focus on spiritual matters. However, for someone like the Founder, who since his youth possessed extraordinary physical strength, making one's partner feel technique of the spirit was an extremely difficult thing to do. Hence, many of those who had the opportunity to experience the Founder's technique unfortunately interpreted his

---

*a pen name of the Founder

change of focus to spiritual techniques as simply a change to a softer form of practice.

In 1961, on the occasion of his visit to Kumamoto, the Founder presented to the dojo a brushed calligraphy of the characters "Takemusu Aiki." On the right-hand side of this work is written:

*"A gift to Manseikan Sunadomari Dojo
From Tsunemori,* the mother of Takemusu Aiki,
Springtime of the divine world"*

What does this mean? I think it is without doubt an expression of the Founder's sincere wish as the parent and mother of Takemusu Aiki that, at his pupil Sunadomari's Manseikan dojo, the flower of the way of Takemusu Aiki be opened. Included in this is his invocation that when this flower blossoms, a heavenly springtime will come about and a heaven on Earth will be brought forth.

Fifty years have passed since the art of takemusu was brought into this world by Tsunemori, under the divine guidance of Ō-kami. Thirty years have gone by since Tsunemori, the mother of takemusu, presented the scroll entitled "Takemusu Aiki" to the Manseikan Dojo, and now without a doubt the flower of Takemusu Aiki has blossomed here. The testimony to this is our public pronouncement of the mission of Manseikan Aikido:

*"In the twenty-first century, building a foundation for
the realization of a world of true love and harmony:
Manseikan Aikido."*

FURIMIRU

The dance of falling leaves is a celebration of new life.

DECEMBER 12, 1992

The Founder teaching in the Manseikan Honbu Dojo in 1961.

Harmonious ki is in accordance with the principles of nature; drawing things in through the ki of love is the first principle.

—MORIHEI UESHIBA

A Path for the New Millennium

This year on January 1st, Manseikan Aikido celebrates its thirty-ninth year. During this time the foundation of Manseikan Aikido has been established. I believe that this last year was one in which the finishing touches were put on the foundational building blocks. With the final completion of kokyū ryoku, from this point on, the techniques of Manseikan Aikido will continue to endlessly change based on the groundwork laid out.

Around 1930, before moving to Tokyo at the beginning of the Showa Period, the Founder stopped in the town of Yatsushiro in Kumamoto Prefecture and instructed. During a very busy time before his move to Tokyo, why did he come to Kumamoto?

In 1961, during the Founder's visit to Kumamoto and the Manseikan Dojo, he stayed a night in the Hinagu hot springs area in Yatsushiro. Three people who had received instruction from the Founder during his first stay in Yatsushiro many years before came to pay their respects and spoke about his first visit to their town in those days. At that time, I became aware of his stated reason for taking the trouble to come all the way here during that busy time before his move to Tokyo:

> *"This* budō *will flourish from the Country of Fire.* * *Before I leave for Tokyo, I will first begin practice here."*

Some sixty years have passed since the Founder said this, and now Manseikan Aikido has opened the flower of Takemusu Aiki here in Kumamoto. I can say with confidence that the Founder's prophecy has come true. He always said:

> *"This way is a path that everyone should follow."*

> *"Everyone in the world will come to practice it."*

Also in the written words that the Founder left for us we find the following:

> *"The people of the world are all brothers and sisters. We must connect by the string of love. All of the arts are working for the purpose of doing this. We, as Japanese, must teach the world the true spirit of Japan. As Japanese, we must spread the teaching of the true Japanese spirit to the people of the world through the 'bu' path of Aikido. More than thinking of each other as mere comrades, we must come to think of people of the world as one family living under the same roof, and move forward giving help to others when they are in need and receiving help when we are in distress."*

Aikido is the transmission of the true spirit of Japan to the people of the world. This way teaches, through the techniques of Aikido, the way of harmony and the connection of the string of love. I wonder if this truly can be accomplished? Unfortunately, there is a world of difference between the Founder's purpose of Aikido practice and the Aikido that is commonly practiced today.

---

* an alternate name used for the Kumamoto area

After the war, the Founder preached about the spiritual technique of Takemusu Aiki, but many of his students left out the spiritual component, and in the quest for strength they focused only on haku or the physical component and technique. The problem with a quest for power of a solely physical nature is the same as the impasse or ceiling reached by today's modern society focusing only on the material, physical science, and the like. In other words, it is equivalent to reaching the halfway point on the path and then completely losing direction.

To harmonize with our partner and connect with them through the string of love, we have to awaken their emotions. If we don't transmit this love to our partner's heart through physical technique, then the meaning of Aikido is lost and what we practice has no real significance. Reaching a level that allows one to completely harmonize with one's partner and through technique awaken their emotions is extremely difficult. However, if we faithfully practice every day focusing continually on harmony and becoming one with our partner, such a level will eventually manifest. This is precisely what the Founder refers to by his words, "Aiki is love."

Manseikan Aikido has finally arrived at the fulfillment of these words. When more people have learned to express this true love through physical technique and shared it with the people of the world, then the way of Aikido will continue to spread throughout the world—true to the words of the Founder: "This is a path that everyone should follow."

One of the Founder's poems or songs of the way states:

> Aiki, the power
> born of the oneness of all.
> Those who walk its path:
> Never fail in your struggle
> to hone and refine yourselves.

There are seven years remaining until the dawn of a new century. In today's world it seems as though there is no end to the chaos. Where will the human race be at the start of the new century? It appears as if we are still groping our way through the darkness without any light. The New World, building a foundation for the realization of a world of true love and harmony: Aiki Manseido. It is my hope that those who train in Aikido will ceaselessly continue to aspire to put this into action.

FURIMIRU

Entering inside your opponent the instant you are touched is being there first in heart and mind.

JANUARY 11, 1993

The Founder smiling during a social gathering at the Manseikan Honbu Dojo in 1961.

Each and Every One of Us Is the Savior

For what purpose was Aikido brought into this world? Most of the people practicing Aikido do so without truly knowing or understanding it.

Aikido is said to be good for self-defense. It is evidently also a good method for staying healthy. It is also excellent for the cultivation of spirit. It seems that people begin to practice it for these and other reasons. These views are a reflection of the motives and goals of different kinds of people. However, these are not the purposes of Aikido. Aikido may fulfill these objectives for many people, which is fine, but this is only a small part of it.

For what reason do we eat? Many people eat a meal without giving it any thought. I eat because I feel hungry. In that case, when you become full, is that enough? People's bodies not only become weak due to an unbalanced diet and lack of nutrients, but they can become unhealthy due to excessive eating and drinking. Eating is not solely for the purpose of satisfying our appetites. It is a fundamental root of our existence as humans. Eating, if done incorrectly and not in harmony with its true purpose, can bring negative results. Although there exists a variety of reasons for practicing Aikido, doing so without knowing its true purpose is in many ways akin to this. Essentially, such practice is in error.

So, what is the true purpose we are aiming for in the practice of Aikido? I believe that by reading the recorded and written words of the Founder of Aikido, one will come to understand this. Among these words is the Founder's explanation that: "Aikido is both martial art and religious faith."

Can it not be said that the essence of religion is faith in the divine and teachings that lead humanity toward goodness and virtue? The Founder of Aikido always said that through the practice of Aikido we aim to build a paradise on Earth, and he never neglected to offer prayers to God every morning and evening. The mission of the Founder of Aikido's divine revelation is expressed in "The Spirit of Aiki Manseido." This "great spirit of love and reverence" of which the Founder spoke is not a concept that is easily understood through simple contemplation.

Many of the Founder's doka [poems of the way] deal with the heart and spirit of Aikido. Following are a few of them:

> Set in motion
> the power of the cosmos
> by wielding Aiki:
> Create a beautiful world,
> and foster peacefulness.

> The source of Aiki,
> flows from the power of love:
> With this as the core
> love shall spread through the world
> flourishing endlessly.

> Aiki, the power
> born of the oneness of all.
> Those who walk its path:
> Never fail in your struggle
> to hone and refine yourselves.

Aiki, protector
of the manifest world,
and the divine path.
Aiki's role in the world:
To cleanse and preserve the Earth.

Looking at the world,
weep not in desperation.
I am moved to bravery
by the wrath of God.

Unite Heaven and Earth,
God and man in harmony
all linked together.
Protect the reign [of the divine].

The way of aiki,
cosmically boundless:
For the multitude,
becomes illumination,
opening up the whole world.

Grand techniques of ki:
Bringing calm to the spirit,
tools of purification.
Kindly offer us guidance,
God of Heaven and Earth.

All of these poems express hope and prayers for the mission of
Aikido.

Now at the dawn of a new century, talk of the end of human
existence can be heard. There is no other path to proceed on but

that which we as the human race create. However, it is common knowledge that throughout the history of the human race, many prophets have preached the way, speaking as the voice of God and Buddha, giving warnings to humanity. Between fifteen hundred and twenty-five hundred years ago, figures such as Buddha, Christ, Confucius, Lao-tze, Mohammed, etc. were all espousing fundamentally this same teaching. Speaking from a general perspective, these prophets in their respective time periods felt that the human race was in crisis. They taught that if humanity fails to amend and change its spirit, God's "final judgment" (according to Christianity) and Mappo no Yo (Buddhism) will come about. Even in twentieth-century Japan, new religious movements such as Kurozumi-kyō, Tenri-kyō, Konko-kyō, and Omoto-kyō emerged as divine signs from the heavens. It should be known that the Japanese people received divine signs and admonitions from God between the end of the Edo Period and the middle of the Meiji Period. Below is one such admonition written in the Meiji Period on February 23, 1903:

> *"The reason that the divine world of the past was so serene and tranquil was that all people were blessed with gentleness and possessed the heart of God. However, the world became dark, people's hearts turned evil, and not an iota of the heart of God remained in their hearts. In the course of time this gave rise to a world in which people put themselves above God and forgot the presence of the Divine. I [the deity] am toiling hard so that I shouldn't have to sacrifice even one individual, yet if the hearts of the inhabitants of the world become all the more rotten, there is no telling what will occur. Be aware that I wish to transform the world and will do what has to be done, be it eradication of the world or reduction of the populace. Please caution others about this."*

"A divine world is one in which humans come to foster the heart and mind of God. When humans come to develop such a state, God will take care of them, providing for their needs. However, one mustn't desire to do things according to one's own devices; this will lead to nothing."

These are fairly gentle warnings, yet there have also been some much more severe. Such admonitions to the human race from heaven have all but been exhausted. Humanity is continuing to move deeper and deeper into a world of darkness. Just where on Earth can help be found? There is no other way to salvation than for each and every one of us to awaken to this and individually endeavor to refine and polish our spirit. More than fifty years ago, the spirit of Sarutahico Ō-kami [the gods that serve as guardians for the community] guided the Founder in the creation of the techniques of takemusu. God spoke to him, telling him to devote himself heart and soul to techniques of the spirit and the martial art of takemusu. If Aikido techniques don't center on the spiritual and don't focus on unification of mind, spirit, and body, then they are of no help or salvation to the world. Moreover, if each and every one of us isn't ready to become its savior, then the human race on the verge of its extinction cannot be resurrected.

FURIMIRU

The bottoms of our feet support our whole body and perform many functions. By massaging them well and taking care of them, they will happily maintain your health.

MARCH 11, 1993

The Founder giving a demonstration at the Fukuoka Assembly Hall in June of 1961.

The Spirit of Heaven and Earth

It's December and the year is drawing to a close. Many things occurred on Earth during the course of this year. The events were not particularly different than those of years past, but when they occur in close proximity to oneself it makes an especially strong impact. The power of natural phenomena and disasters such as earthquakes, tidal waves, floods, and typhoons is unfathomable in proportion to the power that human beings possess.

Unable to comprehend why such disasters occur, human beings may only begrudge Heaven and begin to hate the Earth. As human beings living on this Earth, are we merely at the mercy of the infinite flow of the universe? Bear in mind that humanity's feelings toward Heaven, Earth, and Mother Nature are a reflection and manifestation of our spirits. If we feel that nature is wonderful, it is wonderful indeed, but if we have hateful feelings toward nature then nature appears to be a devil wreaking havoc on us.

In the midst of the flow of the eternally infinite universe, the result of how we handle things—in other words, the approach taken by us humans living on the Earth this instant—manifests itself. If our Earth and universe are truly wonderful, then the approach of humans in the past was good, and the opposite would occur if the approach had been bad. It is perhaps an accumulation over thousands of years. Heaven, Earth, and Mother Nature provide all the necessities for humanity's existence, including the wisdom and intelligence required to sustain life. This wisdom, when functioning properly, includes the realization that Heaven, Earth, and Mother Nature are splendid; but when out of order, the state of the Earth too goes haywire. This means that bad or evil wisdom has gained strength.

Forty years have passed since November 23, 1953, when I held the first public demonstration of my immature and unskilled Aikido. Since this time, I feel that it has blossomed wonderfully. Morihei Ueshiba is the father who gave life to what we know as Aikido. That life inherited from the Founder has blossomed and flowered. It is the spirit of love and reverence for all things. The spirit of the universe is this love and reverence for all of nature. Those who are attempting to hinder and destroy the Founder's heavenly technique are the devil. This devil is none other than the selfish ego that leads people's hearts down the wrong path. Through an unguarded opening one can easily become possessed. This is the path of self-destruction.

FURIMIRU

When you hit a wall in your training and start losing interest, quitting for a while only serves to strengthen that wall. The key to overcoming this barrier is to persistently continue your training and stay on the path.

DECEMBER 11, 1993

The Founder in front of the entrance to the Manseikan Honbu Dojo in 1961.

The Founder and the author in Kagoshima, October 1963

Throughout human life, there is endless adversity. Overcoming it adds a noble flavor and a zest to life. The bird comes and cries; that is the harmonious tying together of God's ki.

—Morihei Ueshiba

Present Heart and Mind

If asked "What are you thinking about this very moment?" you would probably be able to give a pretty clear answer. Your thoughts are perhaps related to your hopes for the year or dreams of the future. Among these may be thoughts that are continuations from last year and even brand new ideas born just this year.

Without a doubt, people are always thinking of something. The famous French scientist Pascal said, "Man is but a reed, the most feeble thing in nature, but he is a thinking reed."

Present heart and mind. The condition of the heart and mind of each and every one of us is in constant flux and capable of instantaneous change. If we consider for a moment that the occurrence of natural phenomena on Earth is directly correlated to the states of people's hearts and minds, then the state of our hearts at the present time is something extremely important and not to be ignored.

Delight, anger, sorrow, pleasure—the entire of the myriad of thoughts and feelings that occur in our hearts—can have good or bad effects on the world around us. People's hearts and minds are much like the branches and leaves of a tree, which are vigorously shaken by big gusts of wind and lightly swayed by gentle breezes.

Similarly, the variety of occurrences around us cause people's hearts to shake or sway. This leads to upheaval and disorder in society. Yet the difference between the wavering of people's hearts and the shaking of the branches of trees is that in the case of individuals, something that may have an emotional impact on one person may have absolutely no effect on another.

People's hearts, much the same as a tree, also have a base and roots, which is a person's spirit. Thus depending on the individual, people react differently to a variety of situations. If the roots of a tree are strong, even a typhoon cannot blow them over. The same holds true for one's spirit if it remains firm. A firm and stable heart cannot be uprooted by trifling matters.

Looking at the world today, we see many people who despite being of high social status become entranced by money and as a result fall prey to self-destructive behavior. This comes about due to an unsteady heart and an unforged spirit. Forging one's spirit is of fundamental importance in leading a full life. However, in order to polish our spirit we must establish a clear-cut purpose for life, or the spirit cannot truly find peace.

The creation of a wonderful paradise on Earth is the true purpose of the human race. Amongst the Founder's written words are: "completing our mission in life by instilling in us a love and reverence for all of nature." I believe that making this spirit of love our own and aiming to incorporate this spirituality into our day-to-day lives eventually leads to a state in which our hearts will be refined and at peace.

FURIMIRU

The state of your heart today is proof of where you have been and how far you have come on the path.

JANUARY 11, 1994

The Founder and the author in Kagoshima in October of 1963.

The Path to the Pinnacle

Life's journey begins with the utterance of one's first cry at birth. Because we are born, we are destined to continue living. This is, put simply, setting your sights on life's pinnacle and continuing to tread the path in front of you.

Just what is life's pinnacle? Life's pinnacle is our final destination point, death. Although each person's pinnacle differs, no one but perhaps God knows where or when one will arrive there. At some time or another, everyone reaches this pinnacle, but until one actually arrives there, one doesn't know what kind of place it is. The point that one reaches is individual, and no two are alike. When thinking of this pinnacle as the top of a mountain, it must be kept in mind that this pinnacle is not always up but may also be under the earth in total darkness.

When climbing a mountain, each step must be taken carefully and firmly. A little carelessness can cause a slip and a fall into a ravine. But putting this aside, the feeling one gets after finally reaching a mountain's peak is truly magnificent. People endure pain and difficulty and continue climbing the mountain in order to be able to feel this magnificence. Life's pinnacle is much the same in that if one aspires to reach a magnificent pinnacle, one must do so step by step and remain diligent through the pains and the hardships of life's journey.

Just what is the magnificence of life's pinnacle? In the world there are all kinds of teachings of the way that one can follow. Yet not all of these are guideposts that lead to a magnificent place. Why is this? Despite the existence of a variety of wonderful ways to reach this magnificent place, it is up to our actual actions as individuals to put these teachings into practice. For example, disposing of trash on the street and in public places is an act that everyone knows is wrong, but despite knowing this, not everyone puts this into practice and the streets remain dirty. Everyone is given a conscience with which to judge right and wrong. At every moment, every day of our life, one's conscience is either working properly or lying dormant.

What is life's purpose? The purpose of our lives is creation of a wonderful world on the face of this place humanity calls home, Earth. As human beings born onto the Earth we must make this our aim and goal. The basic foundation of this movement is the spirit of which Aikido Founder Morihei Ueshiba spoke with the words: "the completion of our mission in life by instilling in us a love and reverence for all of nature." Doing so is not a difficult thing. It is in each moment of time that we live, how we handle events and the continuous occurrences of our daily life in accordance with and true to our conscience. The accumulation of this forms the path that leads us to the pinnacle and collectively builds a platform for the construction of Heaven on Earth.

FURIMIRU

It is okay to set your sights on the techniques of your seniors, but you must not forget to gaze further in the distance towards the pinnacle, embodying the spirit of "Aiki is love."

FEBRUARY 11, 1994

54 ∽

*The Founder demonstrating at the Shinbukan Dojo in
Kumamoto City in 1961.*

The Founder speaking at the Shinbukan in Kumamoto in 1961.

In knowing true Aiki, age disappears. Reaching a deadlock based on the lower self is proof of inadequate training, which brings about old age.

—Morihei Ueshiba

The Last Five Minutes

The year is A.D. 1994 of the Christian era, a system that is now in common use throughout the world. How many years have passed since the beginning of humanity's existence on Earth is not known with precision, but without a doubt we are now living in a technologically advanced and modern age. After thousands of years, humanity has finally reached a point where it can be said that the world has become a smaller place. We are living in an era of continuing advancements in science, one where information is available to us around the world in real-time. With all this progress, one cannot help thinking that we are extremely blessed to be living in such a time. Yet, how many people alive today are truly living their lives conscious of this? Probably most of them don't give this any thought and fail to feel anything special about the time in which they live.

The history of the human race is riddled with conflict and war. Throughout the ages, the strong have preyed on the weak, and wars have occurred ad infinitum. Unfortunately, this remains true today. Despite ongoing progress in science, the advancement of civilization, and the quality of people's lives said to be at an all-time high, people's hearts are increasingly dominated by selfish desire and greed.

The beginning of the Christian era is linked to the birth of Jesus Christ. "Christ" is the Greek word for "savior." His teachings have been spread widely and there are hundreds of millions of followers throughout the world. There remain only a few years before we mark the year 2000 in the Christian era. Yet even despite our society becoming more scientifically advanced by the minute, there are still millions of people on this Earth suffering from malnutrition, dying of starvation, and without shelter and a home to call their own. In light of all this, can we really say that the world is at peace? Racial conflicts, religious wars, economic warfare, and a variety of other bloody conflicts with self-serving motives continue. Furthermore, recent climatic aberration stands as proof that the pollution and destruction of nature continue as a result of the selfish desires of mankind. Japan has even reached the point where it has to import its traditional dietary staple, rice. Recently there have been editorials about housewives racing around from store to store in pursuit of this once plentiful staple. To make matters worse, things have reached such a pitiful state that there are occasional stories of finding mold in the imported rice or even dead rats. This whole situation is no doubt representative of political and governmental ingenuity.

Religion has lost its ability to comfort and mend people's hearts and has become a mere façade. In the Bible the "Last Judgment" is prophesied, so too in the teachings of Buddhism, referred to in Japanese as Mappo no Yo. Even though throughout the ages there have been many saints, prophets, and wise men who have shown humanity the right path, mankind gets corrupted by the world of selfishness, desire, and ego and goes astray. These prophets admonished that after many years if humanity fails to clean up its act, in the end a severe punishment will be brought down from the heavens by God. However, people continue to turn a deaf ear.

Beginning with humanity's emergence on the Earth, when it is all said and done, how far we come and where we ultimately end up is in fact the "Last Judgment." There are some who may ridicule the idea of a Last Judgment, but each and every person's individual "Last Judgment" occurs not in the manifest world but in the spiritual world where there is no turning back. The Last Judgment here in the manifest world, the world in which we now dwell, has already begun. Some are aware of its existence and some are not. However, when we reach our final stage in life, even a fool can feel and understand this. The year 2000 is just around the corner; we are now into the proverbial last five minutes. What will the final day of the year 2000 be like? This once-in-a-lifetime experience is quickly drawing closer. I believe that the only way to move forward and welcome the new century is to make our life's purpose that of fostering the spirit of love and reverence, and living each day with vigor and to its fullest.

FURIMIRU

In the olden days, people considered smoke from tobacco good for warding off evil spirits and poisonous snakes. Recently, concerns expressed about tobacco's harmful effects are growing. Too much of anything is never a good thing.

MARCH 11, 1994

Where Are You Now?

How many people have been born and died since the seed of the human race was first brought down from the heavens? In the future, how long and to what point will the human race continue to exist?

In contemplating such things, one comes to the realization that the time that we are on this Earth represents only a tiny fraction of an instant in the long history of the existence of the human race. All of the people living in the world today are in the process of dying and will do so in the next hundred years. In another few hundred years, traces of most people's existence will be completely erased and forgotten by history. "For what reason are we born into this world?" If we don't give serious thought to this, the human race will remain only a seed and perhaps perish. God put humans on the Earth; there must be a purpose for our existence. Just what is this purpose?

Many people alive today may think along the lines of: "God did not create humankind. We are simply born here. If we live our life irresponsibly doing only as we please, this is just fine!" However, as beings awarded by God with the highest intelligence and spiritual level among all living things, by thinking in this way the meaning and significance of our gift are lost, and we become more foolish than any other living thing on the face of the Earth. With the exception of humans, all other things existing in nature are functioning with respect to the roles deemed by God. However, the human race at the highest level of all living things and blessed with wisdom and intelligence is losing its spirit. As the use of intelligence to pursue selfish desires continues to take precedence, all living things on Earth are now falling into a moribund state. In fact, we have reached such a state that recently humanity itself has coined the phrase: "The human race is the cancer of the Earth."

Despite occupying what amounts to only an infinitesimal fraction of time in the long history of the human race, people selfishly pursue gratification of self-centered desires, destroying the Earth in the process. Through flesh and body, humans perform actions in the physical world, the world of mankind. It is thought that the physical lifespan of human beings is around 120 years. If a mere 120 years is the extent of a person's world, then is it not an empty thing?

It is commonly accepted that after one perishes, one's soul is released from the body into the spiritual world. Recently, it seems that numerous books concerning the spiritual realm are being published, but there are still many people who continue to deny its existence. The fact that there are such people is inevitable because the spiritual realm is not visible to the naked eye. Despite this, there are many people who feel or have experienced with certainty something intangible and beyond the physical world and who believe that a spiritual realm exists.

The Founder of Aikido, Morihei Ueshiba, was a person who prayed to God every morning and evening, while walking the path of a warrior and training constantly. In his forties, during his period of intense physical and aesthetic training, the Founder was said to have uprooted a tree by himself that thirty people together had previously been unable to move. This incident was actually witnessed by numerous people. In 1961, during the Founder's visit to Kumamoto, while chatting with him after a meal I asked him, "Ō-Sensei, how were you able to lift by yourself such a large tree that thirty men had not been able to move?" Picking up a toothpick, the Founder replied, "It was something like this." It was done with the ease of picking up a toothpick. This was a spirit entering the Founder and lending him power. Using spiritual power the Founder was able to lift the large tree.

There is another story of a similar nature I heard directly from Mr. Chiba, who is now teaching Aikido in America. During a festival [of the harvest] at Kumano Shrine in the city of Shinmiya in Wakayama Prefecture, the Founder was scheduled to demonstrate. However, it rained that day and the stage on which they were to perform was uncovered. So they were waiting out the rain, but since it didn't appear that it would stop anytime soon, the Founder decided to perform anyway. When he stepped onto the stage amidst the rain and began his demonstration, surprisingly, the rain stopped and sunlight beamed only over the stage on which the Founder was demonstrating. Mr. Chiba spoke to me about his feeling astonishment at this miraculous occurrence of that day and about the power of prayer. He had been the Founder's partner during the demonstration that day.

These kinds of occurrences are workings of the spiritual world. They cannot be denied. Naturally, beyond the examples that I have mentioned, many people feel that they have had some type of spiritual experience. Such kinds of occurrences point to the existence of a spiritual world.

Emanuel Swedenborg's Spiritual Diary is quite famous. In it is written that in the spiritual world there exists both a heaven and hell. Depending on the religion, a variety of names are given to these. In heaven, there are various levels separated into lower, middle, and upper, and within these a variety of further groups and levels. Hell has a similar system, with levels that vary depending on the severity of one's vices and indiscretions.

If you consider for a moment that when we die, we pass into the spiritual realm and then enter a level determined by our actions while alive, then we can clearly understand the meaning and importance of our life in the manifest world in which we dwell now. In other words, we can think of the finite world in which we are living as preparation for our entrance into the spiritual world.

Using the physical body given to us, the good acts that we did for the world and the harm that we may have caused, all of our actions in the physical world whether good or bad dictate which part of the spiritual world we will go to after death. I am of the belief that it is for this goal that this world was created. Just how do we define "good" acts? There is no doubt that one can argue endlessly in an attempt to define what is wrong or evil. Shouldn't we look instead at the overall picture and be guided by the light of our conscience in asking ourselves whether we are living our lives in pursuit of self-gratification or doing what we can to make the world a better place?

The hearts of people living on this Earth can be in either an "angelic" or "devilish" state. In an instant, our hearts and minds can flutter back and forth from feelings of goodness and being at peace to having feelings of evil, negativity, and the like. Just as there exist things in life that make us feel at peace, so too are there things that make us feel like acting wrongfully. At this very moment, while we are alive in the flesh and physical realm, we have the freedom to choose between the two and act in accordance with these choices. In other words, we have the freedom to either advance upwards or sink downwards. The present in which we dwell is the manifest world that lies between heaven and hell. Thus, from our current position while blessed with a physical body we have the ability to know both right and wrong, to differentiate between heaven and hell, and to polish and refine our spirit accordingly. When all people of the world awaken to this truth, come to know heaven, and feel at peace, then Heaven on Earth will become a reality. This brings to mind the words of the Founder:

*"Life's true purpose is to build an infinite and eternal
Heaven on the face of the Earth."*

In the eternal stream of human history from past to present
and into the future, as human beings living together on the
same Earth at the same moment in time, if all 5.5 billion of us
don't come to feel a sense of fellowship with other humans, then
endless repetition of conflict, fighting, and war will continue. If
this perpetual cycle of violence continues then the significance of
the role that we are given as the most advanced of all creatures on
Earth is lost. Life is short, so shouldn't we desire to live together
cooperatively, helping one another in times of need?

Ponder for a moment your path toward an eternal life in heaven.
Where are you now? Are you heading in a direction toward heaven
or hell? If you feel that you are on your way to heaven, in what
part of heaven will you arrive, the highest or lowest? While alive
in the flesh, we should aspire to build a stable spirit and elevate
ourselves one step closer or even one level higher in our journey
to heaven. Life is *shūgyō*, a process of training and refining the self
that only ends upon our death. In closing, I would like to call to
your attention another doka of the Founder that reads:

> The physical vessel expires,
> yet the soul lives on forever.
> Because I aspire
> to live on in heaven
> it has made life truly joyful.

FURIMIRU

**Victory over the self is not easy. All you have to
do is look at those around you losing the battle to
understand this.**

Our Sole Possession

In "The Spirit of Aiki Manseido" there is a sentence that talks about "bringing our hearts into oneness with the spirit of the universe." I believe that this passage is of extreme importance. The Founder first declares that "Aiki is love," directly following this with the words "bringing our hearts into oneness with the spirit of the universe." This is of great importance not only for those of us who aspire on the path of Aikido but for the entire human race.

Without cost, Mother Nature provides everything for nourishing and sustaining life. This is the spirit of selflessness and all-encompassing, unconditional love. This is the spirit of love and reverence that the Founder refers to. By connecting with this spirit and advancing on a path toward the completion of our purpose in life, we are performing shūgyō on the true path of budō [the martial arts]. Without first fostering this great spirit of love and reverence within ourselves, our mission in life cannot be completed.

The world has become more tumultuous and people's everyday lives have become filled with unhappiness. This is a result of people's consuming pursuit of gratification of selfish desires. Furthermore, conflict that occurs between individuals, war between states, as well as racial and religious conflict are all rooted in the absence of a spirit of loving protection and reverence toward all life.

If the state of people's hearts remains unchanged, then a day of true peace on Earth will never prevail. When people become conscious that the longevity of the physical body and flesh is limited, then they will come to understand that everything, both internal and external, doesn't belong to us. They are vessels lent to us by the God that gives us life. As human beings we are simply granted the use of these vessels.

Saving money and working to achieve wealth are OK, but if it's being done only to satisfy one's own wants and desires then it can become a distraction and hinder the ultimate completion of one's life mission. If God's true intention, as the planter of the seed of humanity on Earth, is the creation of a glorious world here, then mankind must make its aim the orchestration of this and use everything in its power to realize this potential. When all things awaken to this and foster the great spirit of love and reverence, this will become the foundation for bringing about a wonderful paradise on Earth.

In Japanese there is a common expression that building wealth and saving it to leave for the next generation can often result in the inheritors frivolously spending what they have received, not having earned it themselves to realize its true value. Not to mention other unfortunate consequences that often occur in relation to wealth and inheritance such as bickering and conflict amidst family members. Among the teachings of Saigo Takamori is one that says something to the effect of, "For the sake of future generations, don't purchase extravagant land." Furthermore, one of the Founder's doka reads:

> Wealth stored and hid away
> Not used for the world's people;
> This blessing of yours,
> You must decide whether
> It becomes gravel or gold.

If the purpose of our lives is clearly defined, then we ought to take advantage and make use of the individual gifts and talents that each one of us is blessed with to work toward accomplishing this collective goal. When the people of the world advance in unity toward this purpose, then will the power of all things on Earth be harnessed and come forth for its accomplishment.

Nothing in this world is our own. Everything in this world is on loan to us by God for use as instruments for the achievement of our mission in life. In effect, we make use of these instruments to polish and cultivate our spirits and lead us down the ultimate path, the unity of body and spirit, our highest potential as human beings. It is only this soul/spirit that once refined shall go on living eternally at peace in heaven. Aiki Manseido, too, has set its sights on this "spirit of love and reverence for all things" and after forty years given bloom to technique of the spirit.

FURIMIRU

Their purpose served and their mission complete, dead leaves fall to the ground and return to Mother Earth, laying the groundwork for their regeneration.

MAY 11, 1994

The Founder after having paid his respects in front of the miroku statue in Yamaga City, Kumamoto Prefecture.

The Founder in front of Aso Shrine in Kumamoto in 1961.

The ki of love is like the light from the sun;
Left, right, above, below, in front, in back, you must
envelop yourself in it.

—MORIHEI UESHIBA

The Grand Drama of Life

Since mankind made its appearance on the scene, a conclusion has yet to come in this drama starring humanity and set on Earth's stage. As the final scene of the twentieth century draws to a close, no one can clearly predict how this mysterious play will further unfold. Every day the acts of this drama are presented to us through the newspaper, radio, and TV, yet this is representative of only a small portion and not inclusive of all that goes on behind the scenes. The large majority of this is unseen and unheard by humanity and fades into the background.

Just who will take center stage as the leading role performing amidst applause remains unwritten. What is known is that this drama is open-ended and the plot simple, a struggle between good and evil. But no one can clearly distinguish the good from the evil, who will play the role of the villain or the force of good, and what the final outcome will be. All of this will become clear to us only at the time of the final curtain, the Last Judgment. The cast is composed of all of us, the entire human race. What kind of role have you played up until now—the role of a villain or the force of good? Or have you despite your best intentions to play a good role, in fact become a villain or vice versa?

Unfortunately, despite heavy anticipation, the ultimate outcome will only be determinable at the final curtain. Yet the role each of us has come to play will be recognizable when one's soul departs from the physical world on Earth and enters the spiritual world. At this time, God will not be the judge; instead, all that you have done—both good and bad—will become clear in the spiritual world.

While still in the flesh, things may seem a bit ambiguous, but the truth will manifest itself when one reaches a state without a physical body, just the soul. As actors on Earth's great stage, we must be consciously aware that our individual actions can bring about both good and bad consequences, and we should strive to live our lives in a manner cognizant of this. I believe that to truly do so, being aware of the great divine power and sustenance that nurtures and provides us with life is of the utmost importance. By becoming aware that we are not just living but rather are "granted life" by the workings of a divine source, we inspire within ourselves feelings of gratitude toward this magnificent power.

This can take the form of looking toward the sun and giving thanks, gazing at the stars and feeling gratitude, appreciating a drink of water amidst the heat of the day, being thankful for the trees, plants, and greenery surrounding us, and being aware that every breath of air we take in is a blessing. These are all expressions of appreciation for the endless resources lovingly provided by nature that sustain our lives.

We too must foster this same "spirit of loving protection" within our own hearts, saying good-bye to the bad guy inside us and brightly shining in our role as the force of good.

FURIMIRU

We must not forget that God presents us with trials and tribulations to test the strength of our hearts and polish our spirits.

JULY 11, 1994

The Founder cradling the baby of a member of the Kagoshima dojo in 1961.
At left is Fukiko Sunadomari.

You must break free from set form, create, generate, and
evolve. Takemusu is both vast and subtle.

—MORIHEI UESHIBA

Understanding Gratitude

This year saw many people badly in need of water and in distress
due to drought. In situations like this, before we even start to feel
an appreciation for water, we often begin to wonder why it won't
rain for us, and inner voices of resentment toward Heaven begin.

Last year due to damage from unseasonably cold weather and
the ensuing poor harvest, riots occurred and many people felt
frustrated, cursing nature for seeming to hold out on us with the
blessing of the sun's heat.

Just as there are many who never truly appreciate their
parents until they have passed away, many people only come to
truly appreciate peace after they have experienced the misery
of war. Feeling gratitude and thankfulness, even if momentary,
is something we generally experience not during normal times
but rather during troubled times or when something out of the
ordinary occurs—hence the writing of the word "thankfulness" in
Japanese using the kanji characters for "to have" and "difficulty/
distress." This points to the sensation that we feel in times of
distress when we truly come to understand our blessings, realize
the true value of things to us, and gain appreciation for them.

Yet after the storm blows over and things return to normal, many people tend to forget that anything happened and lose this sense of appreciation. There is an expression in Japanese describing this tendency that says, "Once it passes your esophagus, the heat is forgotten" (referring to people's tendency when eating something extremely hot that burns their throat to forget the pain as the food reaches their stomach and continue eating). Of course, it is perfectly alright for us to put our hardships and difficulties behind us and move on, but that being said, it is ignorant to fail to recognize the importance of life's basic essentials such as the sunlight, water, and air provided for us by Mother Nature. Worse yet is neglecting to express our gratitude for these things in our daily lives that are so often taken for granted. Prayers of thanks to the divinefor Mother Nature's blessings are a fundamental expression of the spirit of gratitude.

Among the recorded words of the Founder of Aikido, Morihei Ueshiba, is the following:

> *"All things on Earth are a function of universal love, therefore the true unification and harmony of all things is the spirit of the universe. Each and every person must endeavor to realize and carry out this mission. Aikido is the way that brings to fruition the true spirit of universal harmony and is the only path for bringing the universe into accord."*

The Founder further stated:

> *"Performing technique in harmony and accordance with the principles of the universe is essential. This is none other than fostering a sincere spirit. Progress and advancement in* budō *training will fail to come if one remains self-centered, relying only on ego. This kind of* budō *is misguided and will inevitably turn back upon one's self, bringing about misfortune. Instead, one must form a sincere, harmonious connection with the ki of the universe*

(ki-musubi), *not becoming caught up in the feeling of concern for immediate victory or defeat. When feelings and intentions remain bound in the physical body, there is no rebirth and no regeneration. Things first come to life through harmonious union. Through this harmonious unification, feelings and intentions transform to divine power and all things become clear."*

What is this "ki-musubi" of which the Founder spoke? I feel strongly that "ki-musubi" is sincerely connecting with the heart of our partner through the techniques of Aikido. By endeavoring every day to accomplish this and continuously devoting ourselves, it is possible to form a connection between ourselves and the people of the world. This, in turn, will bring about the fulfillment of what the Founder spoke of by his words:

"This budō *is a path that everyone should follow."*

At the Aiki Manseido Dojo, we continue to pursue realization of the Founder's way of harmony as expressed by his words: "The unification and harmony of all things is the spirit of the universe. Each and every person must endeavor to realize and carry out this mission."

It is only now, after many decades of practice, that I finally have come to deeply understand that this way of Aikido created by the Founder is the true path to creating a wonderful Heaven here on Earth. For this I am truly grateful. It is only after continuing to walk this path and finally reaching the truth that one sincerely comes to appreciate this way.

FURIMIRU

Greeting a perfect stranger with "good morning" and receiving a friendly reply in return is the creation of the unified connection of musubi.

OCTOBER 11, 1994

It is not established that the large will be victorious over
  the small;
The small accumulates and becomes big,
The big breaks down and becomes small.

—Morihei Ueshiba

A World of Different Viewpoints:
Seeing, Hearing, and Interpreting

There are roughly 5.6 billion human beings living on the Earth, meaning that there are 5.6 billion individual lives. Each person's way of life differs, based on the nature of all that person has seen, heard, and received. In the olden days, information was limited, and people's thinking was confined to what they observed and heard in close proximity to them. In today's modern age, we live in a time where unlimited information is at our fingertips, and we have come to think about things from a much broader, worldly perspective. Yet even brothers and sisters born under the same roof, raised the same way, and brought up in the same environment develop different styles of thinking and living. Phenomena such as this clearly demonstrate that each person is born into this world with his or her own individuality. At present, in the field of education, the ideal method for bringing out, nurturing, and developing each person's individuality is a widely discussed topic. The Founder, Morihei Ueshiba, is responsible for the creation of Aikido, but much like other ways and teachings, depending on how his students receive, interpret, and internalize these teachings, various changes and forms can come about.

A state in which all 5.6 billion individuals can take full advantage of their distinct personalities, allow them to bloom, and in doing so live a complete life, is proof that a fantastic world has become a reality. The reason for much of the dissatisfaction of people today is that not all people receive the opportunity to fully give life to their individuality.

Some people are of the belief that it is just fine if they choose to walk life's path doing only as they please. Yet I wonder if, from the bottom of their heart, these people are truly content with this approach and can say that they are joyfully making the most of each day. That being said, the idea of giving life to individuality is not the same as living frivolously and selfishly. It is discovering what you are best suited for and doing your part for society according to your own individual abilities and personality traits. After all, even the construction of a beautiful single-family home can only be completed thanks to the balance and fit of the unique properties of a variety of materials.

The Founder of Aikido clearly taught the purpose of Aikido practice in his words, "Aiki is love. It is the way that brings our hearts into oneness with the spirit of the universe, to complete our mission in life by instilling in us a spirit of love and reverence for all things." Making the Founder's teachings the aim of one's Aikido training should, in the end, lead down the same singular path, arriving at a way of harmony and musubi that recognizes no enemies and is free from animosity. Yet, depending on how one sees, hears, receives, and interprets his teachings, one can end up going in a completely different and misguided direction. There aren't supposed to be different kinds of Aikido; there is truly only one. Likewise, humanity has only one ultimate aim, to build a great paradise on the face of our planet, Earth.

Life changes depending on our way of looking at
things, listening to things, and taking things in.

NOVEMBER 11, 1994

The Spirit of the Universe

"All technique should be completely in accordance with the true principles of the universe. Technique that is not performed in accordance with these principles will turn back upon one's self and lead to self-destruction. This kind of martial technique cannot create a connection to the universe and thus is not the martial art of takemusu. A martial art that connects us to the universe is also one that connects human beings on a horizontal level through the blessing of love. Therefore, this martial art that connects us to the universe is takemusu no bu."

"Performing technique in harmony and accordance with the principles of the universe is essential. This is none other than fostering a sincere spirit. Progress and advancement in budō training will fail to come if one remains self-centered, relying only on ego. This kind of budō is misguided and will inevitably turn back upon one's self, bringing about misfortune. Instead, one must form a sincere, harmonious connection with the ki of the universe, not becoming caught up in the feeling of concern for immediate victory or defeat. When feelings and intentions remain trapped in the physical body there can be no rebirth and no regeneration. Things first come to life through harmonious union. Through harmonious

unification, feelings and intentions transform to divine power and all things become clear."

At the beginning of the year, I jotted down two or three of the Founder's recorded teachings to ponder. Through these words, just what did the Founder intend to transmit to us after his death? If these ideas are not correctly communicated and passed on to further generations, then Aikido will move away from the path that the Founder intended and will become something entirely different.

Whenever the Founder lectured, he always focused on getting across the spirit or the heart and mind of the universe. Among his teachings is his affirmation: "All things on Earth are a function of universal love; therefore the true unification and harmony of all things is the spirit of the universe. Each and every person must endeavor to realize and carry out this mission. It is Aikido which is the way that brings to fruition the true spirit of universal harmony, and it is the only path for bringing the universe into accord."

I wonder how many of those who practice Aikido around the world are doing so every day to consciously help bring to fruition the true harmonious spirit of the universe. Unfortunately, it seems to me that the majority of practitioners are not even aware of the Founder's written words and continue practicing in a way more focused on physical destruction than on the harmony of which the Founder spoke.

To mark the occasion of its twentieth anniversary on May 11, 1973, the Manseikan Dojo began its publication of a monthly newsletter in order to pass on the teachings of the Founder, Morihei Ueshiba. This year marks the forty-first anniversary of our dojo and the twenty-first anniversary of the newsletter. During this time, I have attempted to publish in the newsletter those words of the Founder that can be easily understood by the average person. The contents of these newsletters always deal with the heart and mind of the universe and the spirit of Heaven and Earth. Aikido is a way of merging ourselves with and embodying the heart and mind of the universe and the spirit of Heaven and Earth.

It is my hope that those who pursue the study of Aikido deeply read and attempt to understand the words that the Founder left for us, and that they endeavor to progress even one step closer to his spiritual ideas and vision.

After forty-one years in search of this spirit, it is my belief that Aiki Manseido Aikido has finally arrived at a stage that demonstrates an understanding of the spirit of harmonious union among all people and all things. All that remains in continuing to pursue the spirit of the universe is the eternal path that lies ahead of us.

FURIMIRU

Hurdles in your practice cannot be overcome without having sincerity of purpose.

JANUARY 11, 1995

The Founder at a shrine near the top of Mount Aso in Kumamoto in 1963.

In the Flash of an Instant

On January 17, 1995, at 5:46 A.M. in Kobe, Japan, a great earthquake occurred that left an emotional impact felt by all and had great effect on everyone. In the flash of an instant, the fierceness of Mother Earth and the frailty of human life were revealed. The emptiness revealed by the loss of all of one's worldly possessions, which take a lifetime to acquire but only a second to destroy, became painfully evident for all to see. Both the goodness and the evil that exist within people's hearts came to the surface, among other manifestations that emerged as a result of this tragedy.

Why is it that this time the eyes of the world were so focused on the disaster in the city of Kobe? Natural disasters have throughout history continuously wreaked havoc on humanity. Yet in the past, such disasters were isolated, as they were only known to those who experienced the effects directly. However, this time, the realities of the instantaneous destruction of a modern city were delivered to the eyes and ears of the people of the world on the same day.

In an instant, with the destruction of skyscrapers and crippling of expressways, the lives of many people existing at the height of modern material civilization were forced to return to a primitive state.

At such times when the basic essentials of life such as food, clothing, and shelter are in short supply or threatened, people often lose their human-like calm and without a thought for anything or anyone else swarm to the available sources of food and nourishment. Day by day, the voices of those in need of water and food become louder and louder. When something once readily available disappears in the blink of an eye, it is then that people come to discover its importance and come to know and experience gratitude. However, at first there is usually no room for such feelings in our heart. Out of mere desperation and thinking of nothing else, we do everything and anything to search for these essentials. It is only after finally coming to acquire that which we were searching for that we feel a sensation of warmth in ourheart and for the first time feel a sense of gratitude toward and appreciation for what we have.

Cultivating a heart that recognizes the value of things previously taken for granted is important. Just as there are people who come to understand this feeling through direct experience, there are many who come to understand it through images alone (television/media). Conversely, those who despite having been in such a position yet feel nothing at all have lost touch with their humanness and think no differently than a beast.

This century has been witness to a great amount of flooding throughout areas in Europe, the United States, South America, etc., which has no doubt served to cleanse and purify much of the harm done by mankind. It may even seem as if the Last Judgment is upon us. Just why is it that a "Last Judgment" brought about by God has been prophesied? Ever since the birth of mankind, throughout time, people's hearts have become increasingly drawn in by evil, and the human race has proceeded to damage the body of God—the Earth. Throughout the ages, God has sent individuals as divine messengers to warn those who have forgotten the presence of God in their hearts, but the human race fails to listen. Consumed with greed and materialism, it appears that we have reached an end. Yet we must understand that this "Last Judgment" will be brought down upon us not by God, but rather by humanity as we lead ourselves down a path of self-destruction that we created.

The highest path that we can walk is to live life with gratitude in our hearts, consciously aware that nothing in this world is our own, and all things are provided for us by the great God that gives us life.

FURIMIRU

Walk with your head in the clouds and you will stumble and fall. Walk with your head down and you will bump and bruise your head. You should always try fostering a mindset that can see in all directions.

FEBRUARY 11, 1995

Being in a state of bliss free from the self is the essential principle of the martial arts.

—Morihei Ueshiba

What Is Shūgyō?

Yesterday, while listening to a broadcast on Japanese radio of a recital of poems written by children, I received a strong impression from one particular poem. It was written by a five-year-old child and here is a summary of it: "Inside me I have good hearts and bad hearts. There are about two hundred of them and they are always fighting. When my bad hearts win, my mother gets mad at me, but she doesn't know that inside me my good hearts are saying I'm sorry."

Despite its brevity, I think that this poem is wonderful in that it really manages to directly convey what goes on in people's hearts. It demonstrates that even the heart of a child of five feels the internal struggle between right and wrong, and at the same time a drive toward self-searching and self-reflection.

Since childish acts and misbehavior are usually just part of the process of children's development of their abilities, one often need not get upset. Yet, what about adult parents doing the scolding? Littering of public places with trash, empty cans, cigarette butts, etc., occurs daily. Looking at simple acts like these, one can't help but think that such things are manifestations of adults who should know better than children (succumbing to their "bad heart") and are further evidence of a lack of self-reflection on their part.

Recently, there are many problems in the world that have drawn my attention and made me think further about the meaning of shūgyō. The word "shūgyō" was in the past a Buddhist term explaining the discipline, training, and aesthetic practices of the Buddhist priesthood, as well as the cultivation of the Buddhist teachings of benevolence and the practice of carrying this out through performance of good acts. Later, this word came into everyday use in Japanese to describe extensive training of any type, including in the martial arts. Like many other words, it has moved far away from its original meaning. The word shūgyō that is in common use today connotes something far less difficult than in ages past.

Giving further thought to the concept of "shūgyō," I feel that it applies throughout our lives as we contemplate the importance and meaning of existence and put our thoughts and beliefs regarding this into actual practice. If each person truly has a purpose and mission for which they are given life on this Earth, but they fail to clearly define it, living their lives selfishly doing only as they please, then the world will be thrown into disorder.

Today, in the modern world, thanks to such things as laws, contracts, treaties, pacts, etc., we have reached a point where some stability is finally being maintained. However, we must keep in mind that such stability may not last forever and can collapse without warning at any time. The continuous conflict that occurs in some parts of the world is evidence of this. Human beings, as fellow inhabitants of the same planet, must have a collective purpose. This purpose must be none other than to build an eternal paradise here on Earth. All things should move toward this goal and through education nurture each individual, giving life to their respective abilities to bring to this endeavor.

Therefore, returning to the concept of shūgyō, I believe that the true goal of shūgyō is to foster and strengthen the good heart inside each of us. This makes it habitual through instantaneous self-reflection to judge the good from the bad, to conquer our bad heart through our good heart, and to make the performance of benevolent acts a part of our daily lives.

FURIMIRU

The fact that we have food to eat today is proof that we are given life.

APRIL 11, 1995

The Fulfillment of One's Mission

Intellectually gifted youth make use of their wonderful abilities by setting goals and endeavoring to accomplish them, but if the realization of this potential isn't for the betterment of society, then can it truly be said that they have made the best use of their skills? The intellectuals who gave birth to nuclear weapons are considered to be some of the greatest geniuses of their time, yet if their achievements end up leading to the destruction of humanity, then haven't they acted as instruments of the devil? How people choose to put to use the natural abilities bestowed upon them in the world is the key to both the rise and fall of the human race.

We often hear people say, "That person is really intelligent" or "That person is stupid." All this really has to do with is whether someone has a propensity for learning quickly or absorbing large amounts of information, etc. Yet of greater importance is how their skills are serving society at large. Herein lies the problem with today's educational system, which has become focused solely on getting students into famous schools of higher education, instead of fostering each person's individual abilities for the purpose of developing society as a whole. Shouldn't this be the true goal of education?

The Founder of Aikido, Morihei Ueshiba, spoke about "the completion of our mission in life by instilling in us a love and reverence for all of things." In education, this involves consistently stressing and nurturing this "spirit of love and reverence for all things" while simultaneously developing intellect. This fosters the mutual growth and development of both intellect and spirit, or the "perfection of self." Focusing on knowledge and intellect alone and neglecting the spiritual gives birth to people such as those responsible for the sarin gas attacks that occurred in Japan.

Those people who before passing from this world feel that they have used all of the abilities bestowed upon them to contribute to the advancement of society and lived a wonderful life in the process have probably fulfilled their mission. I wonder how many people have felt this way? Moreover, there are probably many people who despite never having had a sense of calling have felt that they lived a wonderful life and passed away peacefully. Everyone's way of coming to grips with their life and finding peace in old age is different. On the other hand, each and every one of us is destined to pass away sometime and depart from the manifest world. Living our days in a slumber, going about our lives until one's dying day without ever giving thought to the meaning of it all, is truly a waste. The Founder said:

> *"All things on Earth are a function of universal love, therefore the unification and harmony of all things is the spirit of the universe. Each and every person must endeavor to realize and carry out this mission. Aikido is the way that brings to fruition the true spirit of universal harmony, and it is the only path for bringing the universe into accord."*

The basis for the "unification and harmony of all things" is universal love. This is the same as the "spirit of love and reverence for all things." The direction and compass course of each of our lives is already set; once we realize this we cannot go astray. When one becomes aware that one's self and all things are unified and of the same body, one awakens to the notion that polluting, damaging, doing harm to others, and harming oneself are in fact the same. Understanding this is the first step toward creating a beautiful heaven right here on the face of the Earth.

The Founder taught that:

> *"Study and training in martial arts is the cultivation of the power of expansion and contraction of the spirit and its implementation."*

In other words, this power derives from actually putting into practice and physically manifesting the spiritual. Fostering a spirit of love and reverence for all things in the core of one's heart and today—in the present moment—putting this into practice is completing one's mission. By holding this love in our hearts and endeavoring to actually carry out our daily lives true to this spirit, we can create inside ourselves the foundation for the materialization of a great world of goodness, truth, and beauty.

FURIMIRU

Physical power succumbs to physical power, but through diligence and effort, the power of the spirit flourishes eternally.

MAY 11, 1995

The Founder demonstrating swordwork at the Manseikan Honbu Dojo in 1961.

Ups and Downs

Watching the high school baseball championships that occur every year in Japan, one often sees the winners raise their arms in celebration while the losers lower their heads in tears—extremely direct expressions of the emotional ups and downs of our inner selves.

In winning, hands are raised and the traditional Japanese "banzai" salute is performed, and in losing heads are lowered and tears of frustration flow. The political elections of late have brought us similar scenes.

The raising of one's hands and lowering of one's head are easily understood visible displays of expression, but these feelings are fleeting, temporary, and nothing more than the falling leaves of a tree. In cheerful times, people raise their heads feeling carefree. In depressing times, people's heads are lowered and they feel gloomy. Perhaps these are extremes of emotion, yet always maintaining our emotional stability is not an easy thing.

In modern times, there is so much stimulation that it is nearly impossible to give our heart and mind a rest. How can we hope to bring stability to ourselves amidst all the restlessness and agitation? Simply becoming accustomed to it and numbing to the stimulation is an approach that doesn't facilitate continual spiritual growth. If we follow such an approach, our life becomes much like seaweed swept up in the wish-wash of the currents and taken from coast to coast and every which-way on a directionless journey.

Each individual has his/her own particular personality traits and abilities, etc.; therefore not everyone can walk the same path. However, the goal of humanity as a whole must be singular and collective. This goal is none other than to create a world of true peace on the face of the Earth. The foundation for the creation of this collective spirit was taught by the Founder and expressed in his words, "Aiki is love. It is the way that brings our hearts into oneness with the spirit of the universe, to complete our mission in life by instilling in us a spirit of love and reverence for all of nature." It is this "spirit of love and reverence for all things" that is the foundation and core component needed to bring stability and tranquility to people's wavering hearts. Some may say that such broad and lofty ideas are difficult to actively implement in our daily life, but it is not really that hard. By simply contemplating our own existence, our origin is easily understood. The air, water, sun's light and heat, the earth, and all its plentiful nutrients are provided and bestowed upon us. Nothing is our own. Through all of these gifts we are given life, and by realizing this we become aware that there has to be a purpose for our existence.

The Founder often spoke of "becoming one with the universe." If every living thing has the same origin, then all things are united and of the same body. Hence, the world should be one of mutual co-existence and mutual prosperity. Why is it that the human race has yet to collectively open its eyes to this? The attitude of concern only for one's country and people is narrow and archaic, but the world has yet to change its ways. Despite its relatively small scale, Aiki Manseido is working on a person-to-person basis to transmit and pass on technique that unifies one's spirit with one's partner.

Through this "spirit of love and reverence for all of nature," we can bring stability to the ups and downs of our heart, helping us attain inner peace and allowing us to move step by step along the path to building Heaven right here on Earth.

FURIMIRU

If we always remember that we are alive and here
for a purpose, we make the most of each day.

AUGUST 11, 1995

Remembering Our Beginnings

We are here today because of our parents. Our parents exist because of their parents. Continuing in this fashion to trace the root of our existence eventually leads us all back to a single origin and source, the parent of the human race, God. This original source is the creator of all things. Seeing that we were born upon this Earth and are given life by this source, the conclusion can be drawn that there must be some purpose or mission for our existence here. Naturally, people are not born here on Earth by their own free will and under their own power. Likewise, our parents too had no control over what kind of child they brought into this world. If such things were possible, parents would create children to their own specifications, and there would be little or no suffering in the world. It is God that decides what kind of child will be born. Therefore, for humans to label a smart child a good child and one of below-average intelligence a bad one is to disrespect God's work. No child is ever born into this world evil. So then, what is responsible for the spawning of evil in society? We must give thought to what is at fault in society today that brings this evil into existence.

Each person is blessed with different capacities and abilities, but nurturing and developing these abilities is the role of parenting and education. In the plant kingdom, there exist plants that grow and develop on their own without limit and also those that, given lots of human care, fail to grow. The same holds true for people; there are those who develop wonderfully on their own, as well as people whose development comes about through the aid, power, and guidance of others. Hence, it is the duty of elders or those who come before to assess, give guidance, and lead the younger generation.

Next year in January is the forty-second anniversary of Manseikan Aikido's establishment in Kumamoto City and the fortieth anniversary of our present dojo. This feeble seed of Aikido that somehow found its way to Kumamoto came in contact with many people. It is thanks in part to those people in the past who gave up and wrote off the practice of Aikido that my modern techniques of today have originated and developed and reached their highest level yet. God provided us with Mr. Nakashima, a benefactor and wonderful man who did a lot to help establish Aikido in the area of Kumamoto. If he had not been in Kumamoto, who knows what would have become of this seed of Aikido.

At the end of the Taisho Period, before beginning to teach his new budō in Tokyo, the Founder first came to Yatsushiro in Kumamoto to teach for about three months. According to one of his students at that time, he said,

> *"This* budō *will flourish from the Country of Fire.* Before I leave for Tokyo, first I will begin practice here."*

Some seventy years later, despite these words being rather unknown for quite some time, true to the Founder's prediction and congruent with his ideals of the true budō, the flower of this seed of Aikido has fruitfully bloomed here in the Fire Country, Kumamoto. I will never forget that the seed of Aikido in Kumamoto owes its beginnings and growth, in large part, to Mr.

---

*This is an alternate name used to describe the Kumamoto area, home to Mt. Aso, an active volcano.

Nakashima and the great number of other people to whom we owe our origin.

Furimiru

In life, much like an obstacle course, obstacles both big and small constantly arise. Overcoming these big obstacles leads to great delight. Isn't this the perfecting of self?

NOVEMBER 11, 1995

TOP AND BOTTOM: *The Founder feeding deer in Nara, Japan, with the author's sister, Fukiko Sunadomari.*

The pattern itself is only secondary. Find the pattern's true meaning, awaken your soul, and gain mastery of the heart!

—MORIHEI UESHIBA

Given the Gift of Life

As a new year unfolds, living things add another year to their life. It is inevitable that one's visible body will decay, wither away, and die. If this is the unavoidable fate and extent of our existence in this world, what an empty thing it may seem. Yet, if one thinks deeply about whether it would be enjoyable to live in this world, say, five hundred or a thousand years, the lifespan given to humans by God seems the most optimum. Currently, the oldest person in Japan is a woman of one hundred and twenty years. She has been in the hospital for twenty years now; it seems that being healthy enough to work past a hundred is just not possible. Life and death must simply be accepted and, discounting for the moment the large number of suicide cases of late, this is something that under one's own power cannot be changed. In the great earthquake in Kobe at the beginning of last year, the Tokyo sarin gas attack, and other such disasters, unimaginable loss of human life occurred. Looking around the world, we see that the number of people who have lost their lives to war and starvation is immense. If we are in fact granted life by the will of God, then it must be concluded that so too is the time we are allotted to live. From this perspective, the loss of life due to accidents caused by humankind may be seen as acts against the will of God.

The dawn of a new century is upon us as the year 2000 in the Christian calendar—a millennial occurrence—is quickly approaching. The coming times may well be a great turning point never before seen in the history of the human race. The outcome is in our hands and depends on how we as humanity treat the Earth that we are blessed with. Will humanity grow and progress, leading itself in a positive direction, or have we come this far only to continue abusing and destroying the Earth until we reach a point that threatens our own existence?

Which direction the human race will take and what the final outcome will be is something of great interest, but when that time arrives we may have already passed away. When people come to understand that the collective state of the hearts of the people of the world is directly correlated to the condition of the Earth, then each and every one of us will aspire to return our heart and spirit to a natural state, like that of a newborn child. Such a mindset harbors no selfish desire and feels only gratitude for the gifts bestowed upon us by God. Such a spirit is one that cherishes and holds the Earth in the highest regard, heartily committed to its eternal prosperity. This brings to mind the words of a fifty-seven-year-old man who lost all of his possessions in the disastrous earthquake in Kobe. He later said that he lost all the things he had worked fifty-seven years to acquire, but in doing so he gained heart. It seems to me that these words precisely demonstrate the state of selflessness and spiritual awakening that people can reap from freeing themselves from wants and desires.

All living things are receivers of the gift of life through the provision of life's essentials. Folding our hands together in thankfulness and prayer to God, the root of our existence and constant source of life, is the powerful basis for creating a new century.

FURIMIRU

In gazing at a white cloud adrift in the pale blue sky, the heart that is enamored by its beauty and inquisitive of the cloud's future course is a heart of purity and perfection.

JANUARY 11, 1996

The Founder during a demonstration at the Taiyo Department Store Hall in 1961.

Giving rise to and purifying the spirit: with freedom, it has no limits. This is the secret teaching of takemusu.

—Morihei Ueshiba

The Meaning of Strength I

In the dojo newsletter number 96, I published an article titled "What is Strength?" Lately, it seems that many people have been asking what methods they should employ in practice to become "strong" at Aikido. I'd like to begin by discussing the meaning of the word "strength." Just what does it mean "to be strong" in regard to Aikido? Without understanding this first, the methods that will allow us to attain such strength cannot be established. Before even this, however, one must begin by understanding the purpose for which Aikido was created. If this is not understood, then the significance is lost.

There is a myriad of meanings for the word "strength." In general terms, it may describe athletic skill, physical strength and muscularity, spiritual strength, or simply the ability to be powerful in combat. The most commonly given definitions of "strength" refer to something impermanent like that of the examples given above. We often hear individuals described using the words: "That person was strong." This implies that now that person is no longer strong. Can such strength really be considered true strength?

To cite a well-known story from Japan's past, there was a highly touted, top professional wrestler by the name of Rikidosan stabbed to death by a petty hoodlum. A similar incident occurred in the days when Aikido was still referred to as "Aiki-Budō." I was an uchideshi [live-in student] in 1942, when a certain person from the Aikido world was killed in Osaka. I received news of the incident by telephone from Osaka. At the time, the Founder was in Manchuria and unable to be contacted. It was during the war, so the incident was never made public. I still remember the words that the Founder sadly remarked to me upon hearing the news: "He was too strong." This person was of such strength that even in the Aikido world today he is perhaps unequaled. When the Founder said, "He was too strong," I believe he meant that he truly felt in his heart that this kind of strength was not "true" strength. I still remember his words even now and deeply feel that this was an important lesson.

What is strength? At this stage in my life, I can say now that a truly strong person is one who in one's last breath and with death imminent can say from the bottom of his heart, "I have lived a wonderful life!" Strength is not an objective concept, but rather something extremely individual and personal. Being called "strong" by a third party and appearing so momentarily in relation to others may seem to be strength, but this is not true strength. As I mentioned previously, this is a general, ordinary strength and not the type of strength that we strive for in the practice of Aikido.

Before he passed away, the Founder of Aikido, Morihei Ueshiba, left for his students words describing the revelation he received from God. These words do not concern physical technique but rather point to the realm of the spirit. Without pursuing the study of the spiritual aspect of the Founder's teachings, we can never achieve what the Founder spoke of, which is the attainment of this supreme state of "unification of our spirit and body under the law of the universe."

The Founder said, "This path is one that all people should follow." This being true, then everyone has the capacity to follow this path to reach the supreme realm. In 1942, when I was alone in the dojo with the Founder, he said to me, "This budō is a revelation from God; if you practice it for three months you will have no enemies under heaven [you will be invincible]." Since I knew that the Founder had studied many aspects of the religious world deeply, I could accept it when he said that his budō was a path received from God, but I could not grasp what he meant by "through three months of practice having no enemies under heaven." Fifty years later, I have finally come to understand what he meant by this. In those days, despite being a young teenager, I was given an extremely deep concept to ponder. These words spoken to me by the Founder have remained a constant support to me throughout my life and even today.

Forty-two years have passed since then. Through chance and a personal connection, I began teaching Aikido in Kumamoto in 1952. In those days hardly anyone knew anything about Aikido. Because the art was quite rare, many people came to watch. In the beginning, with Kumamoto being the place where Miyamoto Musashi spent his final years and home to many other classical martial arts, many high-level martial artists from other budō came to train. However, after learning the techniques to a certain extent, they would quit and leave. I suppose this says something about my level at the time. However, after a while, the coming and going leveled off and the number of people practicing stabilized. Two years after I opened the dojo in Kumamoto, my teaching duties increased, and I gave seminars outside the prefecture in places such as Fukuoka and Kagoshima. As word spread, I was invited to give seminars at various police academies, such as the police academy for the Kyushu region. For most people it was their first encounter with Aikido, so after I explained the technique and allowed them to try it, they would use the techniques of other martial arts they had already studied to determine if Aikido was effective or not. Unlike teaching the students at your own dojo, holding seminars in other areas tends to become much like an open tournament competition situation. Therefore there were always people in the back of the room saying under their breath such things as, "That technique doesn't work." Despite being rather incompetent and immature, I somehow managed to rise above all of that without any major disaster, thanks to having the support of the Founder as well as his insistence that this budō was a revelation from God.

On many occasions in instances when I was grasped strongly by someone much larger than me and completely unable to move, I would precede the technique with atemi [a strike to vital areas] and leave the explanation at that. However, in instances like these, my own immaturity was painfully evident to me, leaving me feeling quite pathetic. When faced with an opponent much larger and stronger, using physical power and just focusing on the technique doesn't work. Yet, simply going limp and using no physical power at all is even more ineffective. In that case, should those physically weaker simply resign themselves to the idea that they are no match for someone stronger and larger? Of course not. Simply doing so is failing to understand the purpose of Aikido training. Among the caveats of Aikido training is: "Begin each and every practice with tai no henko, every day becoming increasingly more adept at using your body efficiently, such that even in old age, you can continue to practice joyfully and realize the goals of your training." Beginning each practice with tai no henko [body change] suggests that learning to turn the body [referred to as tai sabaki] is of utmost importance. Regarding tai sabaki, the Founder stated: "When faced with one opponent, treat him as many; when faced with many, treat them as one." In the study of tai sabaki, there is no set way to do this. Through daily practice, one will gradually become able to move naturally in such a manner.

For me, personally, the most difficult techniques are those in which we allow our partner to strongly grasp our wrists. There is a variety of such attacks in Aikido, for example katate-dori, ryote-dori, katate-no-ryotedori, and so on. As mentioned before, I often used atemi when grasped strongly by someone and unable to move. However, by remaining satisfied with this, technique will never improve.

Through many years of experiments, tribulations, and lots of trial and error, I came to the realization that this was not a problem that could be solved through mere refinement of physical technique or technical skill. The solution lies not in the physical but in the realm of the spirit. This being said, embodying spiritual principles through physical technique is something extremely difficult to accomplish.

FURIMIRU

Gratitude is conscious awareness of the great power that gives us life.

MARCH 11, 1996

*The lower spirit is winning by fighting, the higher spirit
is winning without fighting. The heart and secret of the
martial arts lie in winning without fighting.*

—MORIHEI UESHIBA

The Meaning of Strength II

In the late 1950s and early 1960s, during a period of struggle and great difficulty for me, the Aikikai Headquarters began publishing a newsletter called Aikido Shimbun which contained the Founder's dowa or "Lectures on the Way." Although these writings were quite difficult to comprehend, I decided to put all of my heart into reading and studying them deeply. The first issue was published April 10, 1959, and on May 10 of that same year, the second issue containing "The Secrets of Aikido" was made available. Following is a summary of what I felt were the important points of this particular writing.

> *"The secret of Aikido lies in cleansing and purifying
> the evils within oneself, harmonizing oneself with the
> movement of the universe, joining with it and becoming
> one. Those who have grasped and internalized these
> principles contain the universe within them, just as in 'I
> am the universe.'"*

> *"How do we clear away the evil ki within ourselves,
> cleanse our heart and mind, and put ourselves in accord*

with the universal rhythm of all things? To do this, we must first make the spirit of the universe our own."

"What is the spirit of the universe? It is an all-encompassing love that extends in all directions, exists at all times—past, present, and future—and extends throughout every corner of the universe."

"Love knows no conflict and has no enemies. The spirit of the universe is a spirit that recognizes no enemies and enters not into conflict. One who acts in discord with the spirit of the universe cannot harmonize with it. One whose spirit is not in tune with the spirit of the universe cannot harmonize with the movements of the universe. The budō *of one who acts in discord with the movement of the universe is the* budō *of destruction and not true* budō."

"A martial art in which there are conflict, winning, and losing is not true budō."

"True budō *is masakatsu gakatsu katsuhayabi* and thus it can never be defeated. In other words, to be invincible is to never give any opposition or fight. To be victorious is to win over the conflict that resides within our own heart, defeating the urge to fight with others; and to carry out and accomplish one's God-given mission."*

These passages were all from the second issue of the Aikido Shimbun. The next few passages are summaries of important points taken from the 104th issue of this same newsletter. It was entitled "Putting into Practice the Resonance of Universal Structure" and came out on March 10, 1969, about one month prior to the Founder's passing.

---

*These words translate as: true victory, self-victory, swift day of victory.

"Everything is to be learned from the universe, united with its center, and assimilated into it. In addition, one must advance in unison with it. In doing so, one correctly weaves the structure and fabric of the universe in one's own body. Fully absorb the resonance of the universe's spirit into your body and mind and harmoniously link with it. The proliferation of this will harmonize the hearts of the people of the world—in other words, connecting through harmony and unification. It goes without saying that this means eliminating war, fighting, and conflict. Everything is musubi, tying together and connecting through harmony and unification. This is Aiki."

Allow me to further offer some straightforward expressions by the Founder:

- Love is the primary ingredient in the creation and nurturing of all things. The ki of love is the center joint in the linking of Aiki.

- Commit yourself to awakening to the importance of training your spirit. Even if you have the form, you will reach a deadlock without training the spirit and will be unable to proceed further. Rather, put your efforts into being born again with an eternal soul.

- Realize that training to overcome the self is of primary importance. The spiritual precedes form. Work hard concentrating your efforts not on form but rather on improving your spirit.

- The lower self follows and the higher self leads. This is the essence of takemusu.

- The lower self (haku) will reach an impasse; employ your pure and intrinsic spirit and devote yourself!

- One must always be resourceful in devotion to the attainment and accomplishment of one's mission, never forgetting this even for an instant.

- Make the higher self (kon) the master and your lower nature its servant, for in being ruled by your lower nature you will reach an impasse.

- Break through kata (set form) based on the lower self and in doing so create spontaneously infinite creations based on the higher self.

- Do not be imprisoned by form; rather endeavor to grasp and embody the true way in both mind and body. In anything that you do this is of the utmost importance.

- Being caught up and imprisoned by kata, one's heart and mind fail to progress. Break free from old forms and craft new forms. Continuously give birth to new forms that are generated in response to the situation at hand. This is the heart of takemusu.In unifying the higher and lower spirit harmoniously, we are given the ability to give birth to truly living techniques.

- In the past people often wondered: "What form is the stance that presents no openings?" Yet, such a stance has no form, instead it is a harmonious state of connection through ki that is given life through the unification of spirit and body.

- Do not be imprisoned by form. You must free yourself from these constraints and make your technique and spirit one. Failing to enter such a state will make the martial arts a weapon of self-destruction.

- Awaken to the essential living mission of takemusu no bu. Remaining imprisoned by set form does not foster progression of the spirit.

- The martial arts are given life through constant change. Takemusu is giving birth to endless innovation evermore.

- Physical struggle and conflict using the lower self bring fatigue and exhaustion without fail. [In performing technique] that gives life to the spirit, one never fatigues.

- There is nothing strange or unusual about teachings of the truth. Seek not the magical and miraculous. By maintaining this state of mind, one can perceive evil spirits, reconcile the inexplicable with one's apprehension, and reveal the truth.

- It is up to humanity as the caretakers charged with governing the order of Heaven and Earth to build a beautiful, ever-flourishing paradise—as well as to ensure the eternal existence of the universe—by laying the foundation for harmony among all people and all living things. This is the path of Aiki that I am communicating.

The expressions that I have presented above are just a few of the teachings that the Founder left for his students that deal with the purpose and goals of Aikido training. If these teachings are ignored and not incorporated into your training, then there is no hope of ever showing any real improvement or progress.

Despite being rather untalented and insignificant, somehow through the pursuit of the Founder's teachings and by endeavoring to embody this spirit in my technique, I have managed to arrive at where I am today, still quite active at more than seventy years of age. In 1972, around twenty years after I began teaching Aikido professionally, I finally came to the realization that this is the essential spirit of Aikido [The Spirit of Aiki Manseido], and I had these words printed and distributed to each dojo, where we began reciting them at the beginning of each practice. I had finally reached a point in my training where I felt and experienced with certainty the deeper meaning behind these words.

The Spirit of Aiki Manseido

Aiki is love. It is the way that brings our hearts into oneness with the spirit of the universe, to complete our mission in life by instilling in us a spirit of love and reverence for all things.

Aiki overcomes self. It not only takes hostility from our hearts, but in turning those who appear as enemies into enemies no more, leads to absolute perfection of self.

This martial art, therefore, is the supreme way and call to unite our body and spirit under the laws of the universe.

A few years ago, there was a young American who practiced here at the Manseikan dojo for two years. Before returning home to the United States, after painstakingly looking up each and every word in a Japanese dictionary, she said to me, "As a Christian, of course I was familiar with the passage from the Bible that states 'Love thy enemy' but I never truly understood what it meant. After practicing Manseikan Aikido I have finally come to understand the meaning of this and have grown to become a much better person. When I first came to Japan, I was spiritually at the level of a twelve-year-old child, but now my spiritual side has finally caught up with my twenty-seven years." Through the practice of Manseikan Aikido, her spirituality and her age finally came to harmonize. Later, there was a twenty-five-year-old, athletic, and extremely powerful young American man who practiced here for one and a half years. Before leaving Japan, he told one of his Japanese training partners, "If these techniques were spread around far and wide, there would surely be peace in the world." Both of these individuals were of the Christian faith and had come to Japan as English teachers. Even where words and languages fail, through the simple touch of a hand the spirit of these techniques of peace can be felt and passed on. I believe these [Manseikan] techniques to be a physical expression of what the Founder spoke of when he said, "Aiki is love." Some fifty years ago, I was told by the Founder:

> *"If you practice this budō for three months, you will have no enemies under heaven."*

After some fifty-odd years, it is only now that I finally feel that I have come to understand the deeper meaning behind these words, which is simply: under Heaven, there exist no enemies. This much can be understood in three months. All that remains is training the rest of one's life to attain a heart and mind like a picture-perfect clear blue sky and reaching a point where one can say, "It has been a wonderful life."

FURIMIRU

A wonderful life is simply on any particular day being able to say, "Today was a wonderful day!"

APRIL 11, 1996

The Founder's calligraphy "Aiki."

The subtle and ever-evolving art of takemusu: to fulfill your destiny through the living ki of love.

—MORIHEI UESHIBA

The Power of Aiki I

What is the power of Aiki? One must first understand the basic underlying principles of this power before one can begin to understand Aikido. At the beginning of the Showa Period (in the mid 1920s) the Founder said:

> *"Aiki derives from the image and spirit of God. It is the spirit that leads to the creation of a world of absolute infinite truth, goodness, and beauty governed by God. Through continuous practice we cultivate virtue and awaken to the truths of Heaven and Earth, thus bringing about its manifestation within ourselves."*

In "The Spirit of Aiki Manseido" these ideas are expressed somewhat differently but in essence point to the same thing. The power used in Aikido is referred to as kokyū ryoku. Exactly when this term came into use I don't know, but it is a word of extreme importance. Kokyū [a word that means "breath" or that connotes "synchronization" in Japanese] is the essential root and basis of all life. It is development of the use of this fundamental power that is the path to perfecting one's self as a human being. This is similarly expressed in "The Spirit of Aiki Manseido" by the words "the supreme way and call to unite our body and spirit under the laws of the universe."

In 1942, when I began practicing, Aikido was at that time called "Aiki Budō." We were given an exercise to develop our kokyū power called kokyūho. However, in those days we simply practiced this as an exercise or kata. No one taught or explained to us just what this power is and how one goes about developing it. I never imagined that by continuing to practice this exercise this power would emerge. At the time, being of small physical size and stature, I was unable to make my technique work when I was firmly grasped by a much bigger and stronger person. The ineffectiveness of my technique was especially evident to me after I started teaching Aikido professionally in Kyushu. Day after day my technique was constantly tested, and yet no matter how much I pursued the physical side of it, I couldn't seem to make my technique work. Some time later, I changed course and began focusing on how to physically express the written words of the Founder regarding spiritual matters.

However, through study of the Founder's writings on spiritual matters and simple imitation of Ueshiba-Sensei—a person known for his incredible physical strength—can a person of average strength really ever hope to develop the same power? Without giving much thought to this, every day I continued to devote myself wholeheartedly to developing technique that expresses the spirit of "unifying with one's partner." After many years of training and study, I was finally able to arrive at a point where I felt that my technique resembled and physically expressed what these words referred to. Whether or not this can be termed kokyū ryoku, I don't know.

When the Founder was in his seventies he said to me, "From now on, I can perform real aiki." I feel that what the Founder meant by this was that the Aikido he performed in the past when he was physically strong was not real aiki, and it was only after he lost his strength that he was able to truly perform techniques with aiki. I believe that the key to attaining kokyū ryoku power can be found in the recorded words of the Founder. About fifteen years back, I published a book entitled Aikido no Kokoro: Kokyū Ryoku [The Heart of Aikido: Kokyū Power]. Looking back on this from where I am today, I feel that it was quite presumptuous of me to have written such a book despite my relative immaturity at the time. Yet, in a way, it became somewhat of a springboard for me to where I am now.

Practicing only the outer form or kata of kokyūho is not enough; doing so is equivalent to performing a stretching routine before attempting to climb a mountain. Without first knowing the entrance to the mountain pass, one cannot hope to advance beyond the mountain's base. Technique is not something that can be understood through discussion and written words alone. The Founder said to me:

> *"No matter how many words are written, no matter how many words are spoken, this* budō *is beyond description."*

Obviously the Founder believed that the depth and significance of Aikido technique are such that it defies description. Yet somehow, I feel that I am at a point now where I have managed to grasp it. All of the recorded words of the Founder of Aikido serve as a guide for the study of Aikido. Following are a few more that I would like to put forth for you to consider.

- The "Aiki" of which conventional martial artists spoke and the "Aiki" of which I speak are fundamentally different in both essence and substance. It is my sincere hope that you will ponder this deeply. Aikido is not the art of fighting using brute strength or deadly weapons, or the use of physical power or deadly weapons to destroy one's enemies, but a way of harmonizing the world and unifying the human race as one family. It is a path of service that works through the spirit of God's love and universal harmony by the fulfillment of each individual's respective role. This way is the way of the universe; the training in Aiki is training in divine technique. Begin to put this into practice, and the power of the universe will come forth and you will be in accord with the universe itself.

- The budō [martial arts] of the past are not sufficient. Up until now was an age of haku [the physical/lower spirit], which only served to build a foundation. In all things one must pursue more than what is visible to the naked eye. Dealing with only the visible never fails to bring about unceasing conflict. Revealing the invisible realm will bring about harmony in this world. Doing this is the only way to the perfection of true budō. The budō of the past was nothing more than the clashing or conflict of set forms and tangibles. With this as the foundation, you must leave it behind you and use the spirit to build upon it.

- It is my wish for all those who forge themselves through Aikido to wholeheartedly devote themselves to fostering universal love and nurturing the spirit of Aiki within their body and spirits; and to use the budō of the past based on haku as a foundation for releasing the light of kon [soul/higher spirit] within themselves. It is my hope that through persistence and tenacity, those who practice will endeavor to make this a reality by grasping the logic of the universe, purifying their hearts and spirits, reaching a state of mind without conflict, and further developing and spreading this great way of Aikido around the globe to bring about an age of peace.

FURIMIRU

Every day people take another step closer on the
path to Heaven or the road to Hell.

JUNE 11, 1996

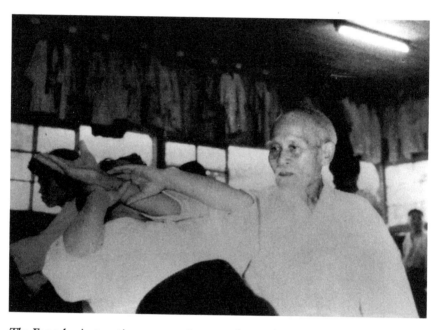

The Founder instructing at morning practice at the Manseikan Honbu Dojo in October 1963.

By unceasingly dedicating yourself, you must seize hold of the truth that lies distant yet within reach and grasp the essence of the spirit!

—MORIHEI UESHIBA

The Power of Aiki II

- When in conflict, harmonize. Five complies with five. Welcome that which comes to you, under no circumstances competing, conflicting, or fighting with it. Instead, like sticky rice cakes, adhere to it and bind with it. When pulled, send it on its way. By unifying your power with that of your partner and becoming one with him, he will come to see the love that you offer.

- The expansiveness of Aiki is vast. The greater one's mastery of it, the deeper it becomes. Let us preserve the well-being of all things so that they can complete their mission and work toward a unified and peaceful world.

- In protecting the body and spirit, it is important that the hands, feet, and hips move and operate in harmony with the mind and spirit. Furthermore, when leading people or being led, the use of the hands is critical. Lead with one hand and control with the other. Endeavor to fully grasp this. The moment that the opponent displays an intention to pull, invite this, giving him incentive and causing in his mind a desire to pull before he has even done so. After one's training progresses, one should be able to simply utilize the deficiencies of one's opponent, recognizing these before he is able to do so. Locate his openings before he does—in other words, uncover places where there are inadequacies and apply technique. The detection of these openings is the way of Aiki.

- Do not limit Aikido to only the present, for in doing so it is not Aikido. Technique improves month to month and year to year. Part of the essence of Aikido is progress, and the changing of techniques over time occurs naturally. I shall stand as your guide for future study.

- All technique is preceded by the spirit. One must never neglect to cultivate the spirit.

- The pattern itself is only secondary. Find the pattern's true meaning, awaken your soul, and gain mastery of the heart!

- The higher spirit is free and empty and the lower spirit has limitations. Yet in coming to know the higher spirit, the lower spirit too becomes liberated.

- Take a mental stance with the ki of love as your primary mindset. This is also training in the mindset of takemusu.

- Even in attaining the state of no-mindedness, if you train properly and practice daily, your hands will move naturally to the vital areas. This comes about as a result of training in divine techniques.

- By connecting and unifying the higher and lower spirit harmoniously, we obtain the ability to give birth to truly living techniques.

- Takemusu Aiki must be the generation and creation of martial techniques. One shouldn't just simply imitate and repetitiously perform the techniques of old.

- Being caught up and enchained by set form (kata), one's heart and mind fail to progress. Break free from old forms and craft new forms. Continuously give birth to new form, generated in response to the situation at hand. This is the heart of takemusu.

- You must make your technique and spirit one. Failing to enter such a state will make the martial arts a weapon that will destroy you.

- Forms crafted by the mind have unnatural components and thus are apt to be easily penetrable. Furthermore, when the unplanned arises, crafted form will be defeated. In divine techniques there is nothing unnatural, and by obeying and conforming, they will not be defeated.

- The lower spirit is winning by fighting, the higher spirit is winning without fighting. The secret of the martial arts lies in winning without conflict.

These are just a few sayings that the Founder left for us. His words clearly establish that Aikido is not the study of a way to down an opponent through physical power and succumbing to the lower spirit. On the contrary, these statements emphasize a way of harmoniously connecting with your partner and joining your higher spirit with that of your lower spirit, bringing them into accord, into a state in which they function in unison. The Founder's statement, "Aikido is love," refers to the harmonious unification of opposites (yin and yang; in Japanese in and yo) and the linking together of kokyū. Those who insist on interacting with others through corporeal power will not be victorious against those who are physically stronger. When allowing your partner to grab your hand, one should do so with the feeling of entrusting yourself entirely to him, creating a connection with him. This kind of power only comes through daily practice and experience and does not reveal itself until one is able to successfully free one's heart from animosity and the perception of enemies. The words of the Founder explain this clearly. He stated that once one has cultivated kokyū [breath power] and reached a level capable of harmonious connection with one's partner, there is no longer need for kata [set form]. From this point on, one reaches a state such as the Founder describes in which techniques emerge freely and form is insignificant.

Based on my experience, I believe that when grasped by your partner, allowing him to feel strong resistance on your part displays your use and reliance on physical power. Whenever I grabbed the wrists of Founder, I never once felt any form of resistance on his part. The cultivation of kokyū power is a state that comes through a lifetime of training and the attainment of the highest level of unity of body and spirit. It is a power that even can emerge from an old man with declining physical strength. After grasping wrists and practicing with as many people as one possibly can, at some point one will reach a sensation of "aha!" I consider this feeling to be the gateway to nurturing kokyū power.

FURIMIRU

Consciousness that all things are sustained and nourished by the same universal parent, God, is the spirit that is unified with all of nature.

JULY 11, 1996

The Founder after having paid his respects in front of the Miroku statue in Yamaga City, Kumamoto Prefecture.

Gifts Bestowed upon Us

The final month of 1997 is here. Every day, unusual events are occurring around us, seemingly without end. Yet the downfall and collapse of human society will be the end. The root of all this is the desolation and despair that lie in peoples's hearts.

We are now living in an age where we can view the Earth from outer space. Astronauts often claim to be deeply moved by the sight of the Earth's magnificent beauty floating in the midst of space. The Earth is the only known planet in the universe inhabitable by human beings, yet why is it that murderous acts and wars occur continuously without end on our unique and beautiful planet? Throughout human history, numerous philosophers and holy men have come into the world and preached about God, the divine, or taught the way of Buddha, yet we are coming to the end of another century without having transformed the depths of these teachings to action or put them to work. The human race has reached a steep mountain pass that we must overcome. By the time we have made it over this pass, humanity may well be on its way toward self-annihilation.

As a human being and member of the human race entrusted with the mission of protecting and guiding the Earth, reflect on yourself for a moment. What are you, really? Why were you born into this world and why are you here? Knowing yourself is, first –and foremost, being conscious that your life is a gift. Making the most of the life we are given entails being mindful that all things that sustain our existence are gifts bestowed upon us by God. Looking at life from such a perspective, one realizes that there must be a purpose for the existence of each and every person on Earth. If one is simply living life for the sake of living, one is living no different than a beast in the wild. The human race must unite with a singular and common purpose. This purpose is to make the Earth into a truly wonderful and peaceful world.

It is my belief that this "completion of our mission in life" of which the Founder referred to is working toward this collective goal using all of the natural abilities bestowed upon us. Living life unconscious of our mission and acting selfishly with nothing but one's own needs in mind gives birth to conflict and war around the world. Moreover, being selfishly absorbed in the pursuit of one's own wants and desires leads to environmental damage and destruction of the Earth. The present state of the world demonstrates what happens when material desires and an emphasis on things of a physical nature take precedence. One need not go any further than the Aikido world to see and understand this phenomenon and its consequences. When one pursues only physical strength, outer form, and technique to down an opponent, Aikido becomes nothing more than a fighting art. Despite coming from the same root, when the purpose of Aikido practice changes it becomes something completely different. The Founder taught that "Aikido is love." In Aiki ManseidoAikido, we have endeavored to make this concept the goal of our training, and the result of this has given birth to technique of unity and a path of harmony.

Using the good spirit within us that we have been blessed with to activate and enliven all living things, we can establish a true paradise on the face of the Earth.

FURIMIRU

On the path to an eternal world we are halfway there. Let's take it easy, not be impatient, and press on.

DECEMBER 11, 1997

The author performing shiho-giri before the commencement of a demonstration.

The author during a demonstration.

For the secret that the warrior seeks: you must know that the basic principles lie in the study of the spirit.

—MORIHEI UESHIBA

On the Occasion of Manseikan Aikido's 45th Anniversary

On January 1, 1954, I began teaching Aikido professionally in Kumamoto City, Japan. At that time, the average person had never heard of Aikido. With the help and guidance of our supporter, Mr. Yoshito Nakashima, and thanks in great part to the cooperation and help of many people, this seed of Aikido planted itself in Kumamoto. After a year and nine months we finally built our own dojo. After establishing a base in Kumamoto City, I began to split my time between training in Kumamoto and traveling around the island of Kyushu holding Aikido seminars for the public. Gradually, the name of Aikido began to spread.

Due to the nature of the martial arts, as one might expect, the measurement of one's strength and superiority is expected and often tested. In tournament and competition the rules are decided, and the determination of victory and defeat is obvious. Yet in Aikido, which focuses on the practice of kata [set forms], the extent of "how skillful one is" often cannot be clearly determined. Herein lies the ambiguity of the practice of Aikido technique.

There is currently a variety of activities practiced under the name of "Aikido," yet within these is a giant gap of difference between the depth and level of technique. Just how can the depth and level of technique really be distinguished? In Aikido, it is simple: one must determine whether or not the physical embodiment of the Founder's words and the manifestation of this spirit through technique are taking place. Expressing this "love" that the Founder described (by the words "Aiki is love") through physical technique is extremely difficult and complex. After forty-five years of daily training and study of the Founder's philosophy, I feel confident that I have finally reached a point where my technique expresses this "love" to which the Founder refers.

> *"In the twenty-first century, building a foundation for the realization of a world of true love and harmony: Manseikan Aikido."*

In these chaotic times, we offer the above statement of resolution to give ourselves a new guidepost for the future. Upon the forty-fifth anniversary of Manseikan Aikido, we changed the name of our practice to "Manseido Aikido." [Manseido translates as "the way of giving life to all things" or "the way for all people."] The purpose and goal of the practice of Manseido Aikido, unlike the majority of the Aikido practiced today, is to correctly pass on the spirit of Aikido's Founder Morihei Ueshiba to future generations.

Lastly, beginning with Mr. Akira Inadome, I would like to thank all those who helped me in each and every way throughout the years and for their generous support during the last forty-five years of Manseikan Aikido. I am deeply appreciative for all that you have done.

FURIMIRU

The impermanent physical body is the tool through which we hone and polish our eternal soul.

JUNE 11, 1999

The Founder and the author standing in front of the Tetori Shrine next to the Manseikan Dojo in Kumamoto.

The Founder and author in front of the dojo.

The author at the monthly yudansha training session at Manseikan Honbu Dojo.

The cycle of the seasons cannot be orchestrated by means of human intellect. It is the work of the divine mind of God.

—MORIHEI UESHIBA

Fifty Years Later, Reflecting on the Start of a New Century

Fifty years from now we will have reached the year 2050. By that time, the youth of today who are now in their twenties will be in their seventies. As people grow older and reflect on the past, they do so from the perspective of the present state of the world around them. Many things occurred in the past that are unimaginable to people today. When the [Japanese] people who are now in their seventies' think back fifty years, they remember a time during the war or shortly after when food was scarce, burnt ruins and devastation were widespread, and suffering was commonplace. Furthermore, in those days many youth in their twenties, both men and women, lost their lives in a war in service to their country. Even worse, in many cases, those who died participated against their will. After losing the war, Japanese society went through tremendous change. The state of society both shortly before and after the country was defeated some fifty years ago was such that even those who were there would have a hard time imagining it today. It was a time when people did anything and everything they could to stay alive.

How does the present age compare? An age has finally come where to a certain extent one is free to think for themselves, and through hard work and perseverance one can accomplish just about anything. This is a year of great significance for mankind. The year 2001 is the first step toward a new era. Just what kind of world will come about? In the coming century, a new world must take shape. We must collectively endeavor to build a world of eternal peace. The practice of Aiki Manseido is a guidepost for the construction of a peaceful world. The Founder stated:

> *"Aiki is love. It is the way that brings our hearts into oneness with the spirit of the universe, to complete our mission in life by instilling in us a love and reverence for all of nature."*

Now I pray for and await the arrival of a future day in which we can say that the purpose that we set and the words that we passionately and wholeheartedly recited daily have become a reality.

FURIMIRU

Days that have passed won't return. Today, in the here and now, is precious.

APRIL 11, 2001

TOP AND BOTTOM: *The Founder demonstrating at the Shinbukan Dojo in 1961.*

The Founder in prayer at a shrine at Oomoto.

Furimiru I

- In Japanese there is a saying to the effect of, "Observe the behavior of others and correct your own." In the practice of Aiki Manseido, one learns by observing one's instructor, assimilating what is learned, and making it one's own. Thus, the job of an instructor is one of great responsibility. Each individual lives one's own life uniquely, dealing with a variety of different situations in a variety of different ways, both good and bad. Observe others, learning from the good that they do and using their bad actions as food for thought to reflect on and examine your own. This state of reflection I term "furimiru," and I regard it to be the way of living life guided by one's heart and mind.

- It is widely accepted that human beings possess what we refer to as a "conscience." Our actions and behavior, both good and bad, our dependent on the state of our conscience—in other words, whether it is weak or strong. Likewise, the reactions and responses that a person's actions bring, whether strong or faint, are a function of conscience. Carelessly discarded cigarette butts in public places are something that people come across every day. Evidence of our "conscience" is this feeling of distaste or unpleasantness that we feel upon seeing such litter. Those who without a thought inconsiderately dispose of such waste without remorse are people whose conscience is weak. Judging from the fact that such acts have become commonplace, I feel that in today's world there are many people whose conscience is in a weak state. If by building a strong conscience we cultivate the self, and this makes us a better person, then shouldn't we endeavor to always examine the world around us, paying close attention to our heart'sresponses? I sincerely believe that making ourselves better is the basis for creating a better world.

- The 1990s are a tumultuous time. In looking at the actions and behavior of numerous nations, it truly makes me wonder what will become of the world after another ten years and how the new century will turn out. The Founder stated, "Aikido brings our hearts into oneness with the spirit of the universe to complete our mission in life by instilling in us a love and reverence for all of nature." Using this as our compass, we must be persistent in keeping close watch on the course that the world is taking.

- When there is an odd number of people in the middle of the cold of winter practice and you are the odd man out, you mustn't sit and rest absentmindedly, for doing so will only make you colder and less inclined to go on. These times are for the practice of *furimiru*. In such times by looking at other peoples technique you can clearly see why their technique failed, for example: because instead of moving forward with their left foot, they did so with the right, or their body was too far away and their balance compromised. Next, when your turn comes and even in using what you have learned from them as a reference, there are times where your technique still fails. It is in times like these that you realize the value of *furimiru*.

- During our black belt training seminars, there are as many as eighty participants in a cramped dojo the size of only forty mats. However, despite the lack of space and people bumping into each other here and there, there is no feeling of unpleasantness. This is because everyone is practicing with the same goal in mind and all of our hearts are in unison. Even with only a few participants on the mat, if one has a heart of animosity and a mindset of conflict, then collision will occur. In unity there is no collision.

- When riding the bus, there are often individuals who, paying no attention to standing passengers, sit shamelessly in two seats or even place their bag on the seat next to them, taking up space. In these situations, the surrounding people often think, "That person is quite rude!" Such intentions and feelings flow toward this individual, blanketing him/her with others' bad thoughts. This is not good. The invisible world of thought and intention can be frightening, and one should always try to do one's best to avoid such bad karma.

- In looking at a single blossoming flower at my feet, my heart feels relaxed and at ease and awakens to the mission of all things. Every tree, plant, and weed has a purpose for which it has been given life on Earth.

- In the world today there even exist people who shamelessly kill their parents for money. People's hearts have become slaves to money, and the world has become corrupt, bearing a resemblance to Mappo no Yo [the Buddhist term for the Last Judgment].

JULY 11, 2001

The author demonstrating at the 297th yudansha training session.

Make yourself one with aiki! This is essential.
If you do not overcome yourself, you cannot overcome
others.

—Morihei Ueshiba

Furimiru II

- When reading the paper, it is always a relief to come across a heart-warming article, like an oasis in the midst of the desert.

- The compass of life resides in our hearts. If one's conscience is clouded, one will soon lose course.

- In the morning give thanks to the morning sun, in the afternoon pray to the dusk-lit sky, on a moonlit night pray to the evening sky, or on a dark night pray to the stars. The spirit of the universe echoes in our hearts, and our clouded hearts are purified.

- The concept that the Earth is sick points to a human race that is sick as well. The idea that our planet is in danger means that the human race also is at risk.

- Simply saying the word "smile" can bring a smile to one's face. Likewise, saying vulgar things gives us a vulgar expression. Words are divine.

- In verbal exchange, as well as physical interaction, if individuals' kokyū don't match, conflict will arise.

- Even if you are shown the way, you cannot arrive there without walking the path yourself.

- When listening, listen. When speaking, speak.

- When you feel the urge to speak unkindly of others, foster a heart that remains tight-lipped. When others speak unkindly of you, foster a heart that turns a deaf ear.

- Among his teachings, the Founder proclaims that all technique must be guided by and embody the spirit, and he urges us to polish and refine our spirit. The techniques of Manseikan Aikido in which we give ourselves completely to our partner—thereby harmoniously connecting with him—are just that.

- Appreciating something after it is already gone is too late.

- The dance of falling leaves is a celebration of new life.

- Entering inside your opponent the instant you are touched is being there first in heart and mind.

- When you have fully grasped and assimilated within yourself the harmonious connection that we practice through Aiki Manseido Aikido, you will come to understand what is real and genuine.

- The bottoms of our feet support our whole body and perform many functions. By massaging them well and taking care of them, they will happily maintain your health.

- Seeing the frail figure of a person walking unsteadily with a cane, I imagine "That will be me someday," and my heart is filled with empathy and compassion.

- Mankind has not evolved from monkeys. However, in the world today, there exist an increasing number of men who are inferior to beasts. If we continue at this rate, we will come to a time when we have no choice but to label mankind a degenerate form of the monkey.

- There is a saying that "seeing is believing." But seeing the kokyū power of Aiki Manseido Aikido is insufficient; one must feel it to believe it.

- Having no enemies under heaven is the spirit of love.

- Like trees that sway in typhoon-force winds, you can absorb the force of your partners without breaking or giving in by completely entrusting yourself to them.

- No matter how much you brighten the inside of a room, it doesn't compare to the light from the sun. Likewise, no matter how much one dresses up and adorns their appearance, it doesn't compare to that which results from polishing one's inner beauty.

- The physical manifestation of "Aiki is love" is only possible when your mindset is one of harmonious connection, and you unify with your partner and become one.

- When you hit a wall in your training and start losing interest, quitting for a while only serves to strengthen that wall. The key to overcoming this barrier is to persistently continue your training and stay on the path.

- The state of your heart today is proof of where you have been and how far you have come on the path.

- It is okay to set your sights on the techniques of your seniors, but you must not forget to gaze further in the distance toward the pinnacle, embodying the spirit of "Aiki is love."

- In the past, people considered smoke from tobacco good for warding off evil spirits and poisonous snakes. Recently, concerns expressed about tobacco's harmful effects are increasing. Too much of anything is never considered a good thing.

- Overcoming the self is not easy. All you have to do is look at those around you losing the battle to understand this.

- Their purpose served and their mission complete, dead leaves fall to the ground and return to Mother Earth, laying the groundwork for their regeneration.

- To truly understand the heart of another person, you need to cleanse your own heart, freeing it from bad intentions. A heart and mind that is clear and unclouded is like a mirror that reflects the hearts and minds of others. Technique is training to become pure and innocent.

- We must not forget that God presents us with trials and tribulations to test the strength of our heart and polish our spirit.

AUGUST 11, 2001

The Founder's calligraphy "Bu No Hikari." This work can be translated as "the (divine) light of the martial arts."

Closing

The true purpose of Budō is expressed clearly in the written words of the Founder. He explained,

> *"The mission of* budō *is to put an end to conflict and fighting."*

I wonder what many of the people who practice the martial arts feel about this statement. Furthermore, the Founder taught:

> *"Aikido is the principle of non-resistance. In being non-resistant one wins from the very start. Those who harbor ill feelings, possess evil intentions, and whose hearts are hostile and antagonistic have lost from the very start."*

> *"From here forward, we must manifest the true spirit of Japanese culture. Furthermore, we must cease in pursuit of power based on the lower spirit, instead activating and giving rise to our higher spirit, and advancing forward based on the principle of non-resistance which neither competes nor collides with our partner. At any rate, this is the part that I am doing to help bring about harmony in the world."*

> *"The changing of technique over time is the essential nature of Aikido."*

In looking at such statements by the Founder, one may feel that they reflect the thought process of an unparalleled individual and speak of things that are impossible to accomplish by anyone other than an extraordinary person such as the Founder. However, the Founder said, "Aikido is budō and religious faith." Hence, those of us who are serious in our pursuit of the study of Aikido must make his words regarding the spirit the aim of our practice, all the while diligently pursuing training in the physical techniques of Aikido. After all, in the words of the Founder it is clearly written that Aikido is "the supreme way and call to unite our body and spirit under the laws of the universe."

Before I began teaching in Kumamoto, while speaking to the Founder privately in Tokyo, he said to me firmly, "There are no head families in budō." I believe that what he meant by this is that the martial art that he created and opened up for us is not one that can be simply passed on to further generations based on the old-style soke system [a Japanese system of succession based on heredity]. Teaching only kata fails in transmitting the spiritual ideas of the Founder and makes Aikido nothing more than an old-style martial art. Thirty-two years after his passing, the Aikido commonly practiced today focuses only on the practice of rigid form. That which the Founder referred to in his statement: "The changing of technique over time is the essential nature of aikido" cannot be accomplished through practice of kata only. In 1982, I published a book entitled Aikido no Kokoro: Kokyū Ryoku, but since that time my technique has greatly progressed. Looking back, I am keenly aware that my technique at that time was simply an expression of where my level was then. Technique will not progress unless one studies the spiritual world and heart of the Founder, all the while continuing to hone one's technique. Without doing so, "the unification of body and spirit under the laws of the universe" is not possible. It is only when physical technique that embodies the spirit begins to spread globally that the world of peace envisioned by Morihei Ueshiba, the Founder of Aikido, will be realized.

In closing, I would like to express my heart-felt appreciation to Dennis Clark for all of his work translating this book. I would also like to sincerely thank Andrew Ellis for writing the introduction and for his generous assistance with the editing. Lastly, I am enormously grateful for the assistance and help on this project from the many members of Aiki Manseido Honbu Dojo.

Aiki Manseido Information

For further information about Aiki Manseido please visit:
www.aikimanseido.com

or send E-mail to:
info@aikimanseido.com

Main Branch Dojo Location
Aiki Manseido Honbu Dojo
Suido-cho 2-2
Kumamoto City, Japan
860-0844